SONGS OF THE SEA

AND

LAYS OF THE LAND

SONGS OF THE SEA

AND

LAYS OF THE LAND

BY

CHARLES GODFREY LELAND

LONDON
ADAM AND CHARLES BLACK
1895

PREFACE

AMONG the songs in this collection are the Brand New Ballads already known more or less to the public, several of them having an American newspaper circulation, while a few are given at times in public readings; since I have learned, for example, that "In Nevada" was one of the stock-pieces of Mr. Clifford Harrison. They now reappear amended and with additions.

In the "Songs of the Sea" the reader will not fail to observe that three or four, such as the "Mermaid" and "Time for Us to Go," are not by me at all. They are sailors' songs of the olden time, introduced as suggestions for other lyrics, as I have indeed declared in the text, and also to aid in the main purpose or idea which inspires the whole collection—they being in this respect like stones from more ancient edifices built into new houses, as was the wont of men in the middle age.

This main purpose was to set forth with scrupulous care, as of a statue photographed from many sides, the mariner of the sailing—not steaming—ship, who is now rapidly passing away, although some tens of thousands of the species are still to be found in the remoter routes of travel. This kind of man should be interesting, because he is almost the only one who is drawn into his calling by a desire to rove about the world and lead an adventurous, reckless, manly life. Into this life entered, I may say, as "vitalising elements," "shipwrecks and disasters of the sea," the extremes of discipline and dissipation, as well as those of cynical scepticism and superstition, the seeing, like Ulysses, cities and men, and the consciousness, so clear to undeveloped minds and smaller natures, of belonging to a "peculiar" class. This I have borne in mind most earnestly, and those who perceive it will also find that in this spirit the following notes and sketches in song illustrate, I trust accurately, a consistent ideal text, and that all the songs unite to form a single poem.

As for the many scraps, "chanties," choruses, sayings, similes, and bits of sea-lore worked up into the lyrics here and there, I make no attempt whatever to indicate what is borrowed; all that I can say of it is, that if the mere gathering the stones is all the merit of making a mosaic picture (as many seem to think), then I could claim little merit for originality. But as this is not a folk-lore book, in which a writer is held sternly accountable "to give authority for every word," and as a mass of notes would have simply defeated the whole aim of the book, I have preferred making myself amenable to the charge of plagiarism to boring my reader—even as an Italian devoted servant of whom I once heard, preferred to be carried off by the police, on the charge of stealing oranges, rather than awaken and disturb his master who could have explained the matter. I can, however, truly say that as regards ideas, incidents, tales, turns of speech and idioms, current sayings, and so on, from poetry down to vulgarity, I have literally taken so much from sailors themselves that the work, if analysed, would be a curiosity of collocation, like the poems made up entirely of proverbs, or the Sermon of Texts.

Here I would mention my obligation to more than one ancient mariner, and specially to my old friend, Captain Stead, now so long a dweller at the Langham Hotel, for advising about, and revising, these ballads. These friends having carefully studied the work and corrected or modelled its every sentence into ship-shape, have been kind enough to assure me that it would hold its own in the forecastle, as a real thing, and not an imitation; which saying uttered in sooth and truth especially by a friend of forty years' experience in sailing-vessels, mostly "before the war," was to me greatly encouraging.

What I have above written of the "Songs of the Sea" is equally true of the other ballads in this volume. They also form a series of eccentric pictures of American life after the war, brought together, not like chance pictures in a scrap-book, but as I before said, to carry out one idea in reference to a special subject. In this spirit and to this end were they written, from current prose tales. Nor have I ever forgotten that there is in them for the future a kind of folk-lore which is never so apparent to those who live in it as to those who inherit it. When I was a small boy, there was in my aunt's kitchen in Milford, Massachusetts, a cheese-knife, which had no special interest to anybody save to me, because it had been the very sword carried by General

Eaton in his famous march over the Desert to attack Algiers. Nowadays it would be greatly prized. So it is sometimes worth while to think of these things which we now possess, and how rapidly they are hastening to become curiosities—I myself having lived to see every object familiar to me in youth become bric-à-brac. In the last age, everything not in the newest fashion was despised—in this there is a highly-cultured class just beginning to show itself beyond the Realists and disciples of Mental-analytical Chemistry, who look alternately at the Past and Future,

> Even as Janus on the Capitol
> Saw all that was or ever yet would be.

There may be a few among the jealous guardians or spokes around the Hub who may demand by what right I invade the sacred precincts of Boston, and sing about its past. Well, my boyhood was half passed in Boston or near it; there the romance of sailor life, which was marvellous in those times, imbued me, and then and there in common with my mates I devoured the *Mariners' Chronicle*, *Shipwrecks and Disasters of the Sea*, *Lives of the Buccaneers*, and listened with avidity to the tales of those who had been on the briny deep. Nearly all my first-cousins had at one time or other run away and gone to sea or taken long voyages. Among the former were Benjamin Stimson, the "S" of *Two Years Before the Mast;* Charles Leland, who afterwards grew like Samuel Jackson to the height of seven feet; and Samuel Godfrey. From these and many more I learned an incredible number of sea stories and songs, none of which I ever forgot, being to an extraordinary degree accustomed to keep repeating to myself these "stranger legends of the olden time." Hence it comes that I have in my mind such vivid memories of the old North End of Boston.

I would say in conclusion what will be apparent enough to many, that these Ballads make no great pretence to be poetry. They consist of incidents or small "motives" cast into rhyme or measure, as the easiest method of giving them a certain value, just as a tune brings out a song. Most rhymers are criticised more or less severely for pretending to be poets; all that I can claim for this volume is, that it is a kind of collection of curiosities which, as they have seemed to me to be worth remembering, will, I trust, be regarded by others as worth reading.

CHARLES GODFREY LELAND.

FLORENCE, 1894.

CONTENTS

SONGS OF THE SEA

LAYS OF THE LAND

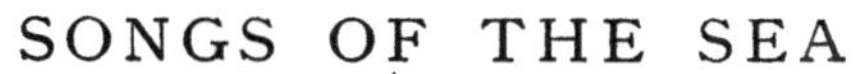

SONGS OF THE SEA

I SAW three sailors synging, hey howe!
  Upon yon lea-land hey!
I hearde three mariners rynging, rumbelowe:
  Upon yon sea strand gaye.
    Synge hey howe, rumbelowe,
    Row the boat, Norman, rowe!

Percy's Relics.

THE OLD TAVERN

IN the North End of Boston, long ago;
Although 'tis yet within my memory;
There were of gabled houses many a row,
With overhanging storeys two or three,
And many with half-doors over whose end
Leaning upon her elbows, the good-wife
At eventide conversed with many a friend
Of all the little chances of their life;
Small ripples in a stream which ran full slow
In the North End of Boston, long ago.

And 'mid these houses was a Hostelrie
Frequented by the people of the sea,
Known as the Boy and Barrel, from its sign:
A jolly urchin on a cask of wine

Bearing the words which puzzled every eye—
Orbus In Tactu Mainet[1] Heaven knows why.
Even there a bit of Latin made a show,
In the North End of Boston—long ago.

And many a sailor, when his cruise was o'er,
Bore straight for it soon as he touched the shore:
In many a stormy night upon the sea
He'd thought upon the Boy—and of the spree
He'd have when there, and let all trouble go,
In the North End of Boston, long ago.

There, like their vessels in a friendly port,
Met many mariners of every kind,
Spinning strange yarns of many a varied sort,
Well sheltered from the ocean and the wind;
In a long low dark room they lounged at ease;
Strange men there were from many a distant land,
And there above the high old chimney-piece

[1] See Appendix.

Were curiosities from many a strand,
Which often made strange tales and memories flow
In the North End of Boston, long ago.

And there I often sat to hear those tales,
From men who'd passed through storm and fight and fire,
Of mighty icebergs and stupendous whales,
Of shipwrecked crews and of adventures dire,
Until the thought came to me on a time,
While I was listening to that merry throng,
That I would write their stories out in rhyme,
And weave into it many a sailor's song,
That men might something of the legends know
Of the North End of Boston, long ago.

First it was said that Captain Kidd in truth
Had revelled in that tavern with his crew,
And there it was he lost the Golden Tooth
Which brought him treasure, and the gossips knew
Moll Pitcher dwelt there in the days of yore,

And Peter Rugg had stopped before the door:
Tom Walker there did with the Devil go
In the North End of Boston, long ago.

Nor had I long to wait, for at the word
Some one observed that he had seen in Spain
A captain hung—which Abner Chapin heard
And said, "I too upon the Spanish Main
Met with a man well known unto us all,
Who nearly hung a Captain General."
He told the tale and I did rhyme it so;
In the North End of Boston, long ago.

EL CAPITAN GENERAL

THERE was a Captain General who ruled in Vera Cruz,
And what we used to hear of him was always evil news;
He was a pirate on the sea—a robber on the shore:
The Señor Don Alonzo Estabán San Salvador.

There was a Yankee skipper who round about did roam,
His name was Stephen Folger and Nantucket was his home,
And having gone to Vera Cruz he had been skinned full sore
By the Señor Don Alonzo Estabán San Salvador.

But having got away alive, though all his cash was gone,
He said, "If there is Vengeance, I will surely try it on!
And I do wish I may be damned if I don't clear the score
With Señor Don Alonzo Estabán San Salvador!"

He shipped a crew of seventy men—well-armèd men were they,
And sixty of them in the hold he darkly stowed away,
And sailing back to Vera Cruz was sighted from the shore,
By the Señor Don Alonzo Estabán San Salvador.

With twenty-five *soldados* he came on board so pleased
And said: "*Maldito* Yankee—again your ship is seized.
How many sailors have you got?" Said Folger, "Ten—no more,"
To the Captain Don Alonzo Estabán San Salvador.

"But come into my cabin and take a glass of wine,
I do suppose as usual, I'll have to pay a fine;
I have got some old Madeira and we'll talk the matter o'er—
My Capitan Don Alonzo Estabán San Salvador."

And as over that Madeira the Captain General boozed,
It seemed to him as if his head was getting quite confused,
For it happened that some morphine had travelled from "the store"
To the glass of Don Alonzo Estabán San Salvador.

"What is it makes the vessel roll? What sounds are these I hear?
It seems as if the rising waves were beating on my ear!"
"Oh it is the breaking of the surf—just that and nothing more,
My Captain Don Alonzo Estabán San Salvador!"

The Governor was in a sleep which muddled all his brains,
The seventy men had got his gang and put them all in chains,
And when he woke the following day he could not see the shore,
For he was out on the blue water—the Don San Salvador.

"Now do you see that yard-arm—and understand the thing?"
Said Captain Folger, "For all from that yard-arm you shall swing,
Or forty thousand dollars you must pay me from your store,
My Captain Don Alonzo Estabán San Salvador."

The Capitano took a pen—the order he did sign,
"O Señor Yankee!—but you charge amazing high for wine!"
But 'twas not till the draft was paid they let him go ashore,
El Señor Don Alonzo Estabán San Salvador.

The greatest sharp some day will find another sharper wit,
It always makes the devil laugh to see a biter bit;
It takes two Spaniards any day to come a Yankee o'er:
Even two like Don Alonzo Estabán San Salvador.

And when this tale was told, another man
Cried out, "I'll swear 'tis true as true can be,
Unto his health we'll have all round a can!
For Captain Folger is well known to me.
Now I will sing 'first lines' of 'Uncle Sam,'
And he who can shall add at once a second,
I'll call you one by one—now here I am,
And he who balks shall be the loser reckoned,
And pay for drinks all round"—
"All right," they roared,
"Now then begin, for we are all on board!"

UNCLE SAM

WHEN there's rain and shine together,
Chorus. Yo heave ho!
Uncle Sam is in the weather:
Chorus. Yo heave ho!

When the sun shines through a fog,
Yo heave ho!
Uncle Samuel drinks his grog:
Yo heave ho!

When the blue sky shows in pieces,
Yo heave ho!
Those are Uncle Samuel's breeches:
Yo heave ho!

When a cloud is low and flat,
Yo heave ho!
That is Uncle Samuel's hat:
Yo heave ho!

When the wind is loud and bad,
Yo heave ho!
Then Old Sam is getting mad:
Yo heave ho!

When the wind begins to bellow,
Yo heave ho!
Uncle Sam is in the cellar:
Yo heave ho!

When the sky is clean and red,
Yo heave ho!
Uncle Sam is gone to bed:
Yo heave ho!

When you hear the wind a-roaring,
    Yo heave ho!
That is Uncle Sam a-snoring:
    Yo heave ho!

When you see the lightning spooning,
    Yo heave ho!
Then old Uncle Sam's harpooning:
    Yo heave ho!

When you hear the wind a-barking,
    Yo heave ho!
Uncle Sam has gone a-sharking:
    Yo heave ho!

When you see a santo-corpus,
    Yo heave ho!
Uncle Sam is arter a porpus:
    Yo heave ho!

When the water gabbles too much,
Yo heave ho!
Uncle Sam is talking Dutch:
Yo heave ho!

When the sea hawk's scream is heard,
Yo heave ho!
He wants to know if there's Dutch on board:
Yo heave ho!

When the wind's before the rain,
Yo heave ho!
Soon you can make sail again:
Yo heave ho!

"Belay that song I say—'tis gettin' weary:"
Cried out a voice, "Let's change to Mother Carey!"

MOTHER CAREY

WITH the wind old Mother Carey,
Yo ho oh!
Churns the sea to make her dairy:
Yo ho oh!

When you see a storm a-brewin',
Yo ho oh!
That is Mother Carey's doin':
Yo ho oh!

When you see Mother Carey's chickens,
Yo ho oh!
Then look out to catch the dickens!
Yo ho oh!

When you hear the icebergs rattle,
    Yo ho oh!
Those are Mother Carey's cattle:
    Yo ho oh!

When you see them split—a-halving,
    Yo ho oh!
Then Mother Carey's cows are calving:
    Yo ho oh!

When you see a flying fish,
    Yo ho oh!
Lose no time but make your wish:
    Yo ho oh!

Irish pennons when they're flying,
    Yo ho oh!
Set old Mother Carey crying:
    Yo ho oh!

When the sea-gulls dip for slush,
Yo ho oh!
Mother Carey stirs the mush:
Yo ho oh!

When one sea-gull follows you,
Yo ho oh!
Mother Carey soon makes it two:
Yo ho oh!

When the sea-gulls fly by two,
Yo ho oh!
Soon good luck will come to you:
Yo ho oh!

When the sea-gulls fly by threes,
Yo ho oh!
Soon you'll have a spanking breeze:
Yo ho oh!

If seven follow you into port,
    Yo ho oh!
There the sailors 'll have good sport:
    Yo ho oh!

When a rope trails in the water,
    Yo ho oh!
That is Mother Carey's garter:
    Yo ho oh!

When the clouds are red as roses,
    Yo ho oh!
Those are Mother Carey's posies:
    Yo ho oh!

If you want to win your Mary,
    Yo ho oh!
Throw out a biscuit to Mother Carey:
    Yo ho oh!

And so they would have chantyd all night long,
But some one broke it with another song.

THE BIRD CREW

THE Albatross
Is the captain and boss,
    Haul away boys, haul away!
The sea-gull queers
Are the officeers,
    Haul away boys, haul away!
And the Carey chickens as I guess
Is every one an A.B.S.,
    Haul away boys, haul away!

"I've heard," said Chapin, "many folk agree,
Those birds are souls of sailors lost at sea,

And often one around the vessel flies
To give us warning ere the storms arise."

"Talkin' of spirits in the vasty deep,"
Said Ezra Bullard, late of Marblehead,
"There's one at least who never goes to sleep,
And mighty little good of him is said;
His special dispensation is to watch
The bottom of the ocean, and to see
It don't fall out—for if it did we catch
The very direst kind of misery,
For all the water runnin' through the hole
Would leave it dry as you can understand,
And from the Arctic to the 'tother pole,
'Twould be one thunderin' lot of empty land."
And thereupon in his south-wester tones
He let us have the song of Davy Jones.

DAVY JONES

Down in the sea among sand and stones,
There lives the old fellow called Davy Jones.

When storms come up he sighs and groans,
And that is the singing of Davy Jones.

His chest is full of dead men's bones,
And that is the locker of Davy Jones.

Davy is Welsh you may hear by his tones,
For a regular Welsher is Davy Jones.

Whenever a fish gets drowned, he moans,
So tender-hearted is Davy Jones.

Thousands of ships the old man owns,
But none go a-sailing for Davy Jones.

"Well—since you talk o' the bottom of the sea,"
Said Enoch Doolittle of Salem town,
"I know a yarn that beats you full and free,
Because, d'ye know, it takes you deeper down,
And if you're taken down—of course you're beat."
"That's so," cried all, "so now your yarn repeat!"
"All right," quoth Doolittle, "I'll serve it hot,
Because, d'ye see, it's called The Devil's Pot.
But 'fore I dive into the salty brine,
Give me a gill of white New England wine!
Take one all round to benefit the pub.
Now for the bottom of the pickle tub."

THE DEVIL'S POT[1]

THERE'S a place where you see the Atlantic heave
Like water boiling hot;
Where you come with grief and with joy you leave,
And they call it the Devil's Pot.

Now there was a witch in the good old time,
And she had such power, they say,
Through rocks or stones or sand or lime,
She could always make her way.

One night on a broom she went with a whirr;
The devil he saw her fly,

[1] The Devil's Pot is a place on the North Atlantic route where, according to sailors, there is always bad weather.

And the devil he fell in love with her
As she went sailing by.

She flew like the devil to scape away,
And the devil so did he,
And she jumped from her broom without delay
And she dived to the bottom of the sea.

And she bored a hole when she got down,
And round and round she twirled,
And closed it behind as she went on,
Till she went straight through the world.

And the devil he dived in the water deep,
And he made it boil like pitch
As he roared and raved with many a leap,
But he never could find the witch.

And still he stirs it by night and day,
And seeks and finds her not;
And that is the reason, the sailors say,
Why it's called the Devil's Pot.

"They say that there are witches everywhere,"
Said Jones of Chesapeake, "a livin' free;
Some in the rocks, some flyin' in the air,
And some, in course, like fishes in the sea.
I've often heard strange voices in the night—
They wan't no birds I'll swer, nor any sitch—
One called me once by name; it gim'me fright—
And that I'm sartin was a water-witch.
One can't in nat'ral wise account for that,
All you can call it is a Mr. E——
But there are witches, I will bet a hat;
And so I'll sing the song of One, Two, Three,
Fust drinkin' all your healths,"—no more he said,
But in a good round voice went straight ahead:

ONE, TWO, THREE

I saw three witches as the wind blew cold
In a red light to the lee;
Bold they were and over-bold
As they sailed over the sea;
    Calling for One, Two, Three!
    Calling for One, Two, Three!
    And I think I can hear
    It a-ringing in my ear,
    A-calling for the One, Two, Three.

And clouds came over the sky,
And the wind it blew hard and free,
And the waves grew bold and over-bold
As we sailed over the sea;

Howling for One, Two, Three!
Howling for their One, Two, Three!
Oh I think I can hear
It a-ringing in my ear,
A-howling for their One, Two, Three!

And the storm came roaring on,
Such a storm as I never did see,
And the storm it was bold and over-bold,
And as bad as a storm could be;
A-roaring for its One, Two, Three!
A-howling for its One, Two, Three!
Oh I think I can hear
It a-howling in my ear,
A-growling for its One, Two, Three!

And a wave came over the deck,
As big as a wave could be,

And it took away the captain and the mate and a man :
It had got the One, Two, Three !
And it went with the One, Two, Three !
    Oh I think I can hear
    It a-rolling in my ear,
    As it went with the One, Two, Three.

This being cheered, I said, "Some time ago
I made a song in the Italian tongue
About a witch and pirate—which for you
Shall, if you like, be now in English sung.
"No, give it first," cried Saltonstall, "by jingo!
In its own nateral, Eyetalian lingo ;
What I don't know of it ain't worth a cent;
Even to Rome I several times have went,
In Naples, too, I've had full many a turn
And know old Spartivento like a dern ;
And most of us, I reckon—though we're Yankee—
Can go the Dago, or some *lingua frankey.*

We ain't so ignorant of what we know;
So go ahead, Signor—*prestissimo!*
Ef we don't catch the sense 'twill be a pity."—
So thus encouraged I began my ditty:

LA BELLA STREGA

ERA una bella strega
Che si bagnava alla riva;
Vennero i pirati,
Lei presero captiva.

Il vento era in poppa,
Sull' onde la nave ballò,
La donna lacrimante
Al capitan parlò:

"O Signor Capitano!
O Capitan' del mar!

Daro cento ducati
Se tu mi lasci andar ! "

" Non prenderò cento ducati,
Tu costi molto più,
Io te vendrò al Sultano,"
Disse il Capitano
" Per mille zecchini d' oro
Vi stimi troppo giù."

" Non vuoi i cento ducati.
Ebben, tu non gli avrai,
Ho un' amante amato
Non mi abbandona mai."

Essa sedé sul ponte,
Principiò a cantar :
" Vieni il mio amante ! "
Da lontano il vento
Si mette a mugghiar.

Forte e più forte
La tempesta ruggio:
Gridava il Capitano:
"Io credo che il tuo amante
E il vento che corre innante,
Ovvero il diavolo."

Forte e più forte
La procella urlò:
"Sono roccie davanti,
E il vento vien di dietro,
Ben venuto sei tu, mio amante!"
La bella donna cantò.

"Vattene al tuo amante
All' inferno a cantar!"
Disse il Capitano,
E gettò la donna fuori
Della nave nel mar.

Ma come un gabbiano
Sull' onde essa voló:
"O mio Capitano!
Non sarai appiccato,
Ma sarai annegato;
Per sempre addio!"

"That's derned good Dago," cried Jack Saltonstall;
Blamed ef I didn't understand it all.
For the best songs are easiest understood:
Now then let's hear if t'other side's as good!
A song is like a bird—'cos birds do sing—
So carve us out the second breast and wing;
And with your anthem bid our hearts rejoice:"
Encouraged thus I lifted up my voice.

THE BEAUTIFUL WITCH

A PRETTY witch was bathing
By the beach one summer day;
There came a boat with pirates
Who carried her away.

The ship had a breeze behind her,
Over the waves went she!
"O Signor Capitano,
O Captain of the Sea!
I'll give you a hundred ducats,
If you will set me free!"

"I will not take a hundred;
You're worth much more, you know:

I'll sell you to the Sultan
For a thousand golden sequins:
You put yourself far too low."

"You will not take a hundred,
Very well then, let them be!
But I have a constant lover
Who, as you may discover,
Will never abandon me."

On the deck, before the rover,
The witch began to sing:
"Oh come to me, my lover!"
And the wind as it stole over
Began to howl and ring.

Louder and ever louder
Became the tempest's roar,
The captain in a passion

Thus at the lady swore:
"I believe that your windy lover
Is the devil and nothing more!"

Wilder and ever wilder
The tempest raged and rang,
"There are rocks ahead, and the wind dead aft,
Thank you, my love!" the lady laughed
As unto the wind she sang.

"Oh go with your cursed lover
To *inferno* to sing for me!"
So cried the angry captain,
And threw the lady over
To sink in the stormy sea.

But changing into a sea-gull
Over the waves she flew.
"O capitain, captain bold," sang she,

"'Tis true you've missed the gallows tree,
But now you'll drown in the foaming sea,
O captain, forever adieu!"

"Talkin' of witches and magicianers,"
Cried out Jack Saltonstall of Newbury port,
"They are the devil's own parishioners,
And I knew one of a peculiar sort,
Because he was a sailor—had he been
A lawyer, now, it wouldn't seem so queer:
For conjurers 'mong us ain't often seen,
And he was of the kind who ain't small beer,
Possessing cash enough to roll in bliss:
However that may be, the story's *this.*"

THE WITCH'S BOX

ONCE when I went upon a trip
Likewise to the Southern sea,
We had a man upon the ship
And a wonderful man was he.

A handsomer man I never did spy,
At home or in any port;
But there was something in his eye
Of a most peculiar sort.

And all in Trinidado's port
Was a woman fair and rich,
With her my messmate did consort,
And I heard she was a witch.

Her eyes, like his, had a greenish glare,
They seemed to be quite of a level,
And the general look of the loving pair
Was exactly the look of the devil.

Now when it was time to up and lift,
And the ship must leave the docks,
He came aboard with her parting gift,
A brown little wooden box.

Now this man had hardly a shirt to his back,
When he started on this trip,
And the mate declared that such a Jack
Was a regular shame to the ship.

Then this man he winked a dreadful wink,
And said to the mate, "I'll be floored:
But I've got more clothes in my box, I think,
Than all of the men on board."

Now his box was only one foot square,
And what was our surprise
When he opened it and pulled out a pair
Of shirts before our eyes!

Next came a hat and a jacket blue,
With trousers of the best,
For everything was nice and new,
And so on with all the rest.

And when he was drest, all spick and span,
We observed upon our oaths
That we didn't believe even our old man
Had got such a suit of clothes.

Twenty-four hours arter, I heard him say,
And I thought it was very strange:
"I never wear my clothes but a day
And now it is time to change.

"I make you a gift on 'em fair and plain,
With a quid of tobacco to boot."
Sayin' this he opened his box again,
And pulled out another new suit.

And the same thing happened the very next day,
At about the very same bells,
He took off his second suit so gay,
And gave it to somebody else.

So it happened every day again,
Till he'd rigged us all from his store;
And such a dandy lot of men
Were never in a ship before.

Then we never had any scrimmages
For fear of spilin' our slops:
We looked like the graven images
Before the tailors' shops.

But a man named Knox from Edinboro toun,
Always took the thing amiss,
And often remarked with a doubtful frown :
"There is something eereligious in this !"

So one day when our friend had opened his box,
Before we could prevent,
Up behind him came Mr. Knox
And dropped in his New Testament.

There came a flash of lightning bright,
And an awful thunder's roar,
And the box and the sailor went clean out o' sight,
And we never beheld 'em more.

And all to ashes and all to wreck
Went our clothes, and we looked forlorn,
For there we were standing on the deck
As naked as we were born !

And this is the lesson short and small,
Which we learned from our liberal friend,
That the things which cost you nothing at all
Never come to any good in the end.

And when the laugh at this had died away,
Mose Brown of Bristol in the whaling line
Said: "Mermaids are the witches of the sea,
Which in good looks are really superfine.
And on this subject I will give a song,
Which I daresay you all already know,
But anyway it isn't very long,
Though it was made a hundred years ago,
I guess that mermaids were much plentier then;
Perhaps they're scared of steamboats and the swell
Which drives the fish as foxes do a hen—
So like the steamers I will now propel."

THE MERMAID

One Friday morning we set sail [1]
It was not far from land,
When I espied a fair mermaid,
With a comb and a glass in her hand.
Chorus. And the raging winds do blow, blow, blow,
And the raging winds do blow;
And we poor sailors climbing up aloft,
And the land lubbers lying down below.

Then up spoke the boy of our gallant ship
And a well-spoken boy was he:

[1] There may be a few readers to whom it is necessary to point out that this first ballad of the "Mermaid" is an old song, here used as introduction to a second by me, which is of the same nature.

" I've a mother and father in London town,
And this night they will weep for me."

Then up spoke the captain of our gallant ship,
And a well-spoken man was he:
" I've a wife who is living in Liverpool town,
A wife whom I never shall see."

" My wife who is living in Liverpool town
This night will be looking for me;
She may look till the sun no more goes down,
She may look to the bottom of the sea."

Then three times around went our gallant ship,
And three times around went she;
And three times around was the end of her trip,
When she sank to the bottom of the sea."

THE MERMAN

THEN another man said when that song was sung:
There are men like you and me,
Who will sometimes come ashore and get sprung,
Yet who live at the bottom of the sea.

For I myself knew one of that folk
(I believe he still lives and thrives),
And I'll tell you the truth without any joke
How we saved one another's blest lives.

I was walking one night in New York town,
And the moon shone bright and clear,
When I thought I heard a singular sound
That came from a board-yard near.

First was a groan of misery,
And then a scythe of pain;
And a voice which wailed: "Oh where is the Sea?
Which I never shall see again?"

And I thought that party must be cracked,
Or a little over the bay;
Because the water was not, in fact,
A half of a mile away.

So I looked that sufferin' mortal up,
And found, sufficiently soon,
A man who looked like a perishin' pup,
As he lay in the light of the moon.

And I said to him, "Matey, just confess
What all of this row's about,
And what was it got you into this mess,
And how can I get you out?"

Then this man he opened his eyes so wide :
" No more do I ask of thee
Than to carry me down to the water's side,
And chuck me right into the sea."

And I says, "'Tis a singular thing to ask,
But I think it can be no sin,
And anyhow 'tis an easy task
To carry and pitch you in."

So I picked that perishin' person up,
And slewed him on my back,
And he wriggled and moved with many a flup
Like a codfish or a jack.

But when I had carried him half the way,
He seemed to be half-way done,
And when we had got 'longside of the bay,
I guessed that his life was gone.

But when he heard the water splash,
He opened his eyes—you bet!
And said: "If you only will make a dash—
Good Lord! there's a chance for me yet!"

And when we came to the water's edge,
I never a word did say,
But carried him right to the end of the Ledge,
And dumped him into the Bay.

And then he gin a yell of delight,
And then he warbled a tune,
As he swam about in the water bright,
All there in the light of the moon.

And he hollered to me his partin' thanks,
And said: "I am outer my pain;
Good-bye! I'm off for the 'Foundland Banks;
Some day we shall meet again."

Now when a year had passed I found
Myself in a Southern sea,
A-wrecked; for all on board were drowned,
And nobody saved but me.

And as I sat upon the turf,
And looked at the water blue,
A man came walking out of the surf,
And says to me: "How do you do?

"I think you don't remember me,
Allow me to let you know
I'm the fellow that you threw into the sea—
In New York—a year ago.

"My home is down in the Ocean deep,
And sometimes—would you think?
I go ashore when men are asleep
To a tavern to take a drink.

"My mother was a mermaid fair,
She lived down in the sea;
And my father he was a Dutch sailór,
So it came that I am what I be.

"And I can walk about on land
Until my clothes are dry,
But that brings up to the end of my sand,
For then I must surely die:

"And my soul sail off for Doldrum Isle,
Unless some one pities my pain,
And carries me down where the waters bile,
And puts me in 'em again.

"One turn deserves another, ahoy!
And John must settle with Jack;
You treated me like a brother, old boy
And now I will pay you back.

"In this bag there is more than a thousand pound,
And I give it all to you:
In a Spanish galloon that money I found,
(It's a thing which I frequently do).

"But in this place you'd be sure to spile,
So now I will give you a tip:
Just walk to the other side of this isle,
And there you will find a ship.

"You'll find her there as sure as you're born;
Her name is the *Clara Belle*,
She sails for Havanna in the morn,
So, matey—fare-you-well!

"Farewell—for here I cannot bide."
He turned his back to the shore,
And walked right into the risin' tide,
And I never beheld him more.

So we never should doubt of a mystery,
There are lots of 'em round us still;
For nobody knows what's down in the sea,
And nobody ever will.

Said Brown, "That story now goes home to me.
Folks say a witch, a wizard, and a Finn,
Are all jint partners in all deviltry,
The Devil himself of course bein' counted in;
And of these Northern conjurers I can sing
A song if you will join me in the chorus.
First take your drinks—that is the prudent thing,
We never know in life what lies before us."
Which having done, himself he did begin
The wondrous ballad of the "Wizard Finn."

THE WIZARD FINN

As I suppose, you all have heard
There's no good luck with a Finn on board,
I can tell you that is so.
I've sailed with one and I ought to know:
    For it is true, upon my word,
    There's no good luck with a Finn on board.

Eric Jansen was his name,
And from Christián' he came;
A seemly man all for to see,
But devil a bit the man for me:
    For it is true, as all have heard,
    There's no good luck with a Finn on board.

From the hour he joined the ship,
All went wrong in all the trip;
'Twas nothing but swear and growl and groan,
And the weather was just the devil's own:
    You may reckon it all absurd,
    But there's no good luck with a Finn on board.

Our grub was spoiled from that first hour,
Except the vinegar all was sour;
All you heard was Lubber! and Liar!
And everything hot except the fire:
    For it is true, as all accord,
    There's no good luck with a Finn on board.

For as the doctors all do know,
A Finn has fins between each toe:
He is web-footed like a duck;
Which is the cause of his bad luck:
    For it is true, as I averred,
    There's no good luck with a Finn on board.

And when at last it got so bad,
That master and men were nigh gone mad,
A rummerin' whisper did begin
That 'twas all along of this here Finn:
    For it is true, and on re-córd
    There's no good luck with a Finn on board.

And the long and short of this debate
Was that one night our second mate,
Bein' as mad as a man might be,
Pitched Eric Jansen into the sea:
    For it is true, unless I've erred,
    There's no good luck with a Finn on board.

When all at once around there came
Over the sea a greenish flame,
And the biggest whale I ever spied,
Rose up by Eric Jansen's side:
    For it is true, as you may've inferred,
    There's no good luck with a Finn on board.

And the Finn he got upon the whale,
And off in the flame we saw them sail;
Hearing a song as they fell behind,
Like women singing with the wind:
    For it is true, as all have concurred,
    There's no good luck with a Finn on board.

Off from the ship and off the shore,
And Eric Jansen we saw no more;
But from that hour, aboard that ship,
All went well for the rest of the trip:
    For it is true, upon my word,
    As you and I have often heard,
    People may say it's all absurd,
    And yet it holds as I averred,
    And bein' a fact it's on recórd,
    Unless the best of men have erred,
    As you may truly have inferred,
    In which observers have concurred:
    There's no good luck with a Finn on board.

"That story of the Finn," said one to Brown,
"Is of the kind which hev been salted down,
Which is the reason, I suppose, why you
Take such a lot of pains to prove it's true.
When tales are c'rect in all their fitnesses,
There ain't no need of forty witnesses,
Nor one at all I guess, but that's enough;
Now listen to the song of 'Charley Buff,'
Who always said, 'I am a truthful man:'"
He polished off his drink and thus began:

CHARLEY BUFF

Oh Charley Buff was his parents' joy,
  And as he always told,
He went to sea as a cabin-boy
  Before he was one year old.

Chorus. Now this is pretty bad,
But it's nothin' to what's a-coming:
Yet Charley he was a truthful lad,
And never indulged in humming.

And this Charley Buff allays said to me:
"To lie I cannot afford,
For you know I hev got more truth in me
Than all of the rest on board.

"I have seen in the isle of Barriboo
Such high-sized coco-nuts,
That the natives used to split 'em in two
And use 'em to make their huts.

"I hev seen the Kanaka women
Foller a ship'n full sail,
A thousand miles a-swimmin'
For a bottle or a tenpenny nail.

"I hev seen the eggs of the toodly-wang;
  It's a bird in the Muldive Isles;
And when they hatch they burst with a bang
  You can hear five hundred miles.

"From a Cariboo king named Jocko,
  A man of cheerful life,
For only a fid of tobacco
  I bought me a beautiful wife.

"One night she was gone, by gum!
  But as soon as ever I missed her,
From the king for a glass of rum
  I bought her younger sister.

"One evening for their tea
  Her family broiled and ate her;
'Never mind!' says the king to me,
  'Just go and pick out a better.'"

Chorus. Now this is pretty bad,
Yet it's nothin' to what's a-coming;
But I hear the old man a bawlin' like mad,
So I guess I will stop my humming.

"Wal," answered Brown, "that comes it rather strong.
Now if you like I'll sing a pirate's song
Of which you all have heard at times a bit;
I've jined 'em into one to make 'em fit,
Like beads upon a string, altho' I fear
It's partly pirate and part mutineer."

BOLD ROBIN ROVER

Bold Robin Rover
   Said to his crew:
"Up with the black flag
   And down with the blue!
Up with the Black Boy!
   All men to show,
Over the water
   And off let us go!"

A man-of-war he hailed us:
   "Come under my lee!"
"See you damned," said the pirate,
   "For I'd rather sink at sea,

In the blue water
 Far out and free,
Cruising down on the shore
 By the coast of Barbary."

We met the *Flying Dutchman*,
 By midnight he came,
His hull was all of hell fire,
 His sails were all o' flame;
Fire on the main-top,
 Fire on the bow,
Fire on the gun-deck,
 Fire down below!

Four-and-twenty dead men,
 Those were the crew,
The devil on the bowsprit
 Fiddled as she flew.

We gave her a broadside
   Right in the dip,
Just like a candle,
   Out went the ship.

We met a gallant vessel
   A-sailing on the sea,
For mercy, for mercy,
   For mercy, she did plea;
But the mercy we gave her
   We sunk her in the sea;
Cruising down on the shore
   By the coast of Barbary,

Four-and-twenty Spaniards,
   Mighty men of rank,
With their golden ladies
   Had to walk the plank,

Over the gunwale
  Into the sea,
Cruising down on the shore,
  By the coast of Barbary.

Oh devil take the captain!
  And devil take the ship!
And devil take the cargo!
  And devil take the trip!
And devil take the bo'su'n!
  And devil take his call!
And devil take the doctor!
  And devil take 'em all!

Over the quarter,
  Over the sail,
Into the water,
  Dead as a nail

Slung like a biscuit,
  Hot as a coal,
Where the sharks may take the body,
  And the devil take the soul!

Then spoke Grim Sam of Jersey, "As we've heard
A mermaid or a witch is the same bird,
But of a different feather, so a pirate,
And slaver, is all one for guards to fire at,
For pirates kill and plunder all they catch,
And slavers at the same are just their match;
There ain't no special difference (it was said
That Sam himself well knew the Guinea trade,
And half-way to the devil had sent his soul
By running into Cuba "sacks of coal")—
And then he sang to us right merrily
A slaver's song, which was not writ by me.

TIME FOR US TO GO

WITH sails let fall and sheeted home, and clear of the ground were we,
We passed the bank, stood round the light, and sailed away to sea;
The wind was fair and the coast was clear, and the brig was noways slow,
For she was built in Baltimore, and 'twas time for us to go.
Time for us to go,
Time for us to go,
For she was built in Baltimore, and 'twas time for us to go.

A quick run to the West we had, and when we made the Bight,
We kept the offing all day long, and crossed the bar at night.
Six hundred niggers in the hold, and seventy we did stow,
And when we'd clapped the hatches on, 'twas time for us to go.

We hadn't been three days at sea before we saw a sail,
So we clapped on every inch she'd stand, although it blew a gale,
And we walked along full fourteen knots, for the barkie she did know,
As well as ever a soul on board, 'twas time for us to go.

We carried away the royal yards, and the stun'sle boom was gone,
Says the skipper, "They may go or stand; I'm darned if I don't
 crook on.
So the weather braces we'll round in, and the trys'le set also,
And we'll keep the brig three p'ints away, for it's time for us to go."

Oh yard-arm under she did plunge in the trough of the deep seas,
And her masts they thrashed about like whips as she bowled before the
 breeze,
And every yard did buckle up like to a bending bow,
But her spars were tough as whalebone, and 'twas time for us to go.

We dropped the cruiser in the night, and our cargo landed we,
And ashore we went, with our pockets full of dollars, on the spree.

And when the liquor it is out, and the locker it is low,
Then to sea again, in the ebony trade, 'twill be time for us to go.
Time for us to go,
Time for us to go,
Then to sea again, in the ebony trade, 'twill be time for us to go.

"Wall," said Mose Brown, "I 'low that that escape
From the derned cruiser was a blame close shave,
And I myself once in as bad a scrape
Was lifted out by one big thumping wave
On the same line of coast—or thereabout,
Since it was off the Bight—that's old Benin—
Where as the sayin' is, 'but one goes out
Of all a hundred strangers who go in.'
It ain't so healthy quite—to be exact—
As 'tis in Colorado high and dry,
Where they send invalids—it is a fact—
Off to some other country for to die;
Excuse me, gents, for keepin' you so long,
Now I'll proceed to let you hev my song."

ROLLING OVER[1]

It was upon a Boston brig, and that was in the Fall,
Our barky she was light as a gig, for our lading was but small;
And it was in the American War as we were sailing thus,
When we saw a steamer from afar, and knew she was after us.

Chorus. Rolling over, rolling over, rolling on.
The roaring waves they came,
Like water into fire all gone,
For the sea was all of a flame.

Now I have often seen by dark the sea a-burning bright,
But nothing did I yet remark like what it was that night,

[1] This ballad was very much revised, corrected, turned over, and re-turned, by sundry old sailors, chief among whom was the ancient mariner, Captain Stead. Almost the same could be said of all these songs, but this one was specially "cut up and salted down for sea use."

And the wake we left behind us as we sailed for many an hour,
Was like a fiery serpent who was chasing to devour.

And then the captain made a speech to us a-standing round,
And said: "'Fore I'll be taken I'll be damned if I don't be drowned;
Yet if you will be plucky, men, and likewise well behaved,
We've got one chance in a thousand yet, but what we may be saved.

"About ten miles to leeward there lies the Guinea land,
And for fifty miles before it clear a narrow bar of sand;
And if we find a deepish place—as such of them there are—
It just is barely possible that we may clear the bar."

Then we gave three cheers for our old man because we liked his dash,
And allowed ere we'd go to prison that we all would go to smash;
So then we set the wheel up with the steamer coming down,
And never a man did care a damn if he was going to drown.

Now as we came unto the bar I happened to remark
A spot among the waves on which the water it was dark;
And I showed it to the captain, who saw the place was fit,
And hollered to the helmsman to steer her straight for it.

Now just as we were working to this very closest shave,
There came by Heaven's mercy a tremendous booming wave,
Which gave the barky such a lift, thanks to our lucky star,
That though we felt the bottom scrape—by God we crossed the bar!

And as we came in the still water we gave three roaring cheers,
For the rebel he was locked outside—of him we had no fears;
But I never shall forget until I come unto my grave,
How we were saved on the Guinea coast by the sea-light and the wave.

Chorus. Rolling over, rolling over, rolling on.
The roaring waves they came,
Like water into fire all gone,
For the sea was all of a flame.

Quoth Nat of Stonington, "That *is* a bruiser,
And yet I know darn'd well it could be done
With the third wave—but talking of a cruiser,
I know a song—'tis just a little one—
But first I would observe that a *muskeeter*
Is not an insect, for as you should know
The term's applied unto a different creeter,
Which sails about the Gulf of Mexico.
Sometimes the thing is called a *guard-accoster*,[1]
And when one did accost us with a gun,
Out of the way we ginerally tost her;
It ain't hard work to make a greaser run.
Well, that'll do. We got a song before us,
And them as likes may holler in the chorus."

[1] *Guarda Costa.*

THE MUSQUITO

SAID Paul unto Peter,
" I see a muskeeter,
        The boat's coming over the bay."
Said Peter to Paul,
" She is saucy, though small,
        And the captain is sailing away."

Said Paul unto Peter,
" Confound the old creetur,
        The boat's coming over the bay."
Said Peter to Paul,
" We will soon make her squall,
        And the captain is sailing away."

Said Paul unto Peter,
" We'll bang her and beat her!
    The boat's coming over the bay."
Said Peter to Paul,
" Set stun'sles and all,
    And the captain is sailing away."

Said Paul unto Peter,
" We'll give her short metre,
    The boat's coming over the bay."
Said Peter to Paul,
" Give her powder and ball,
    And the captain is sailing away."

Said Paul unto Peter,
" We'll roast her and eat her,
    The boat's coming over the bay."
Said Peter to Paul,
" We will gobble them all,
    And the captain is sailing away!"

"Now, 'fore we fairly get into the Gulf,"
Said Saltonstall, "and fall into its tide,
Which swallows up so many like a wolf,
I'll sing a song about a place outside,
Where a thing once took place which was a wonder—
I mean the story of 'Old Stand from Under.'"

STAND FROM UNDER!

I WAS sailing in a vessel a long time ago,
All the while dead against us the wind used to blow,
And it seemed as if aboard us that nothing would go right,
When over the Bahamas a-sailing by the night.
Chorus. By the night, by the night,
When over the Bahamas a-sailing by the night.

In the dark, up in the rigging, or somewhere on high,
"Hallo! Stand from under!" a voice used to cry;

But the Being who hallooed it was always out of sight,
When over the Bahamas a-sailing by the night.

On that gloomy haunted vessel, and all among her crew,
Was a dark and silent sailor whom no one ever knew;
And the Voice it called the loudest when that seaman came to light,
When over the Bahamas a-sailing by the night.

And we said to him one midnight when we heard it worst of all,
"Your friend there in the rigging is giving you a call."
Then he looked up above him with such bitterness and spite,
When over the Bahama Isles a-sailing by the night.

When the Voice with "Stand from under!" once again to him salamed,
He hallooed back like thunder: "Let go then and be damned!"
Like a man in desperation who expects a cruel fight,
All over the Bahamas a-sailing by the night.

And as the word was spoken—like coming to a beck—
A something came a-whizzing and fell down upon the deck,
And the body of a mariner was there before our sight,
All over the Bahama Isles a-sailing by the night.

And looking at the dead man, he said: "I do declare!
An hour's sail from Cuba I stabbed that fellow there.
And now he always haunts me, though I killed him fair, in fight,
All over the Bahama Isles a-sailing by the night."

"But the devil a bit of fear have I of dead or living men,
I've lifted him before and I can lift him up again,
And pitch him in the water, and sink him out of sight,
All over the Bahamas a-sailing by the night."

He grappled with the dead man in spite of all our cries,
When life and awful anger came in the corpse's eyes;
It tore him to the toffrail and held him deadly tight,
All over the Bahama Isles a-sailing by the night.

And overboard together in a grapple went the two,
And downward sunk before us into the water blue;
But in and all around them shone a corpo-santo light,
All over the Bahama Isles a-sailing by the night.

But from that very minute the wind blue well and fair,
And everything went right with us when we had lost the pair;
But I always shall remember while I live that awful sight,
All over the Bahama Isles a-sailing by the night.

"Now that we're gittin' t'wards the Spanish Strand,"
Said Moses Brown, a-waving his bandana,
"I just propose that first of all I land—
As all of us have done—at the 'old Havanna.
Adventures there do gin'rally abound,
The natives being all sus-ceptive creeters;
For if romance upon this airth is found,
It sartinly *is* 'mong the senoritas.
Though he who of 'em would advantage take,

Must be on hand and al'ays wide awake:
Quien el diablo ha de engañar
Mañana ha bien de levantar.
Meanin' that "who the devil would deceive,
Must rise uncommon early," I believe.
That is the precious time to pick a salad,
As happened to the fellow in my ballad;
Who carried off the booty, as the Fox
Took the fair Hen from the two fighting Cocks.

NEAR HAVANNA

It was down near Havanna town, ho!
It was down near Havanna town, low,
That I saw a mortal fight,
At the coming on of night,
By the starlight a long time ago.

Two Spaniards were a-fighting for their lives,
   The blades flashed like lightning up and down;
To the click and the clock of the knives,
   And *there* stood a lady looking on.

I asked her the cause of the fray,
   And she answered in Spanish: "Oh see!
They are villains who carried me away,
   And now they are fighting for me."

And I said as I looked at her face
   That I hardly could blame such a theft,
"But I'll wait until one gets his grace,
   Then I'll tackle with the other who is left."

But just as I spoke, with a start,
   The two leapt and fell on the sand,
For both had been stabbed to the heart
   And each had his death out of hand.

So I and the *donna* were friends,
  And that of the kindest and best;
Now here this true history ends,
  And you must imagine the rest.

And 'twas all near Havanna town, ho!
It was down by Havanna town, low,
    That I saw this mortal fight,
    At the coming on of night,
By the starlight a long time ago.

There sat a stranger there whom no one knew,
Who did not seem a follower of the sea,
And yet no stranger surely to the Blue,
Who now politely spoke the company,
Saying unto them: "Mates, 'tween you and me,
I put it as a question—don't you think
That it is pretty near time to take a drink?
And if you do belong to Gideon's Band,

Then here's my purse to pay—and here's my hand"—
There was a roar of laughter loud and long,
And then the stranger burst into a song;
But for a minute were they all so gay,
For with the words their laughter died away.

THE THREE DEAD MEN

Los tres Muertos

EVER so far and far away,
Down in the hollow by the bay,
Where the beach is dry and the rocks are high,
Under the sand three dead men lie.
    There they lie alow, low, low,
    Nor hear the cockrel's crow.
Where the palm-trees are a-growing, and the wind is ever blowing,
    There they lie alow, low, low.

One was drowned in yonder sea,
One was shot as it may be,
One was left on the beach to die,
But all in the hollow sleeping lie.
    There they lie alow, low, low,
    Nor wake at the cockrel's crow.
Where the palm-trees are a-growing, and the wind is ever blowing,
    There they lie alow, low, low.

Sometimes when the moon is bright
You can see the three, like gulls in flight,
Flitting along above the waves,
Or sitting and talking on their graves,
    Where they lie alow, low, low,
    Nor hear the cockrel's crow.
Where the palm-trees are a-growing, and the wind is ever blowing,
    There they lie alow, low, low.

There was a pause—when some one merrily
Struck up a song which all have known of old;

How Billy Taylor's sweetheart went to sea,
And how she fought in an engagement bold:
And as the talk ran on of female sailors
Who've gone to sea in men-of-war, or whalers,
Until I spoke and said: "I know a lay
About a Spanish lady, old lang syne,
Who, as a sailor, wished to sail away—
The words are by another and not mine:"

THE LADY-SAILOR[1]

I'LL go in yon boat, my mother,
Oh yes! in yon boat I'll go;
I'll go with the mariner, mother,
And I'll be a mariner too.

[1] Irme quiero, madre,
En aquella galera
Con el marinero
Por ser marinera.

Ay, ay, ay, verdadero,
Ay, ay, con el marinero!
And I'll be a mariner too!

Mother, there's no refusing,
What true love demands I must do;
In love there's no picking and choosing,
So I'll be a mariner too.
Ay, ay, verdadero,
Ay, ay, con el marinero,
And I'll be a mariner too!

"I like those Spanish songs," the stranger said:
"Many I've heard and many I have read,
And if you like I'll give you one in rhyme,
By Gil Vincente of the oldest time,
Which holds its own, and bravely, one may say,
For Spanish sailors sing it to this day."

THE SPANISH SAILOR'S SONG

If you're sleeping, my dear,
Wake and open to me!
For the hour is at hand
When afar we must flee.

If your white feet are bare
Still no longer delay;
For deep are the waters
Which roll in our way.

The waters so deep
Of the Guadalquivír;

The hour is at hand,
We must wander, my dear.[1]

'Tis strange, he added, how our land, in truth,
As it goes Southward seems to turn to youth,
And with a softer sun all words are sung—
As things are warmed—into the Spanish tongue:
I've given you a song, let's have another;
"Well, I know one," I said, "which seems its brother,
Although, compared to yours, it's nearer zero,
In Spanish, *Digas tu el marinero!*"

---

[1] Si dormis, donçella,
Despertad y abrid,
Que venida es la hora,
Si quereis partir.

Si descalza estais
No querais calzar,
Que muchas las aquas
Teneis de pasar—

Las aguas tan hondas
De Guadalquivir;
Que venida es la hora
Si teneis partir.

THE LOVER TO THE SAILOR

Now tell me this, my sailor boy,
As sure as you love your wine,
Oh did you ever see a ship
As trim as that girl of mine?

And you who've been in many a gale,
And stood on many a deck;
Oh did you ever see a sail
As white as my true love's neck?

And you who have been where the red rose blows
In many a Southern place,
Oh did you ever see a rose
Like those in my sweetheart's face?

Here's a cheer for the women with jet black curls,
  Of Spain or of Portugal!
And seven for the Yankee and English girls,
  The prettiest of them all!

"Wall now," cried Jones, "I railly must admit,
Them Spanish songs of yourn hev taste and wit;
But as I'm gettin' hungry, what is upper
In me just now is that I want my supper;
And while it's cookin', till they bring the tub,
I'll sing you how a sailor lost his grub."

GREEN CORN AND POTATOES

Oh I once was in love like a sinner,
And the girl she was hahn'some and tall,
She said she would cook me a dinner
Of corn and potatoes and all.

In a pot she put ham and potatoes,
One chicken, and that not too small;
With gumbos and good red tomatoes,
And beans and some oysters and all.

On a rock by the river she cooked it,
When there came up a devil of a squall;
And into the water it hooked it,
With the corn and potatoes and all.

The ham and the beans and potatoes
All went in that devil of a squall,
With the chicken and big red tomatoes,
And carrots and oysters and all.

Then hurrah, boys! Hurrah for the Union!
And the banner which waves from the wall;
Likewise for the parsnip and onion,
Green corn and potatoes and all!

The gumbos, the greens, and the carrots—
Likewise for the monkeys and parrots,
And corn and potatoes and all!

Here John of Baltimore spoke out: said he—
"Mates, you must know I'm goin' to leave the sea;
I've had a fortune left me, as I learn,
So now I guess I give the land a turn.
I am not one who a sea-life belittles,
But do confess I cannot stand the vittles:
You may correct me if you think I'm wrong;
But first I'll give my sentiments in song:"

THE SAILOR'S FAREWELL

HARD tack and cheese, good-bye!
For I am going home,
To keep me warm and dry,
No more on the seas to roam.

Roast beef and turkey free,
And likewise chicken-pie,
Salt junk—farewell to thee!
Hard tack and cheese, good-bye!

I'm going to the land
Where ham and eggs they fry;
Veal cutlets are on hand;
Hard tack and cheese, good-bye!

Roast duck doth there abound,
And mince and apple-pie
In stacks is lyin' round;
Hard tack and cheese, good-bye!

I smell the rich roast goose,
A second slice I'll try;
A third I shan't refuse;
Hard tack and cheese, good-bye!

Planked shad is very fine;
I'm in for living high,
On terrapins with wine;
Hard tack and cheese, good-bye!

I seek my native soil,
For soft-shell crabs I sigh,
And oysters on the broil;
Hard tack and cheese, good-bye!

Unto the canvas-back
Myself I will apply,
And hickory nuts I'll crack;
Of chinquapins no lack;
Hard tack and cheese, good-bye!

The buckwheat-cake shall boom,
The Jersey sausage fry;
Amid green corn I'll bloom,
And hominy consume;
Hard tack and cheese, good-bye!

I see the cranberry sauce,
All with my mental eye;
Plum-pudding I will boss;
Hard tack and cheese, good-bye!

Venison on chafing-dish,
With jelly, by the bye,

Coffee and fresh cat-fish ;
Hard tack and cheese, good-bye !

I'll soon be on the strand
Where luscious reed birds fly ;
My own—my Maryland—
Hard tack and cheese, good-bye !

Old Ocean with thy foam,
For thee no more I sigh ;
For I am going home !
Hard tack and cheese, good-bye !

"That bill o' fare," cried Abner Chapin, loud,
"Is pitched too high for this here Northern crowd :
New England rum, I spose, seems rather meek
'Longside peach-brandy down in Chesapeake.

I don't de-cry your vittles, by no means,
But I prefer a pot of pork and beans
To all the canvas-backs that ever flew,
With soft-shell crabs and reed birds thereunto.
And all burnt offerins of fries of lambs
Ain't worth a dish of good Rhode Island clams;
And all your Spanish mackerel, my man,
Worth one good mackerel caught off Cape Ann!"
"Talkin' of mackerel"—Here Peter Young
Broke off this sermon with the "Mackerel Song."

MACKEREL SIGNS

MACKEREL clouds and mares' tails
  A-sailing, a-trailing,
Make lofty ships carry low sails
  A-sailing, a-trailing away.

When the mack'rel are in the sky,
  A-sailing, a-trailing;
Soon the wind will be blowing high:
  A-sailing and trailing away.

When the mack'rel shine in the moon,
  A-sailing, a-trailing;
Then the wind will begin to tune:
  A-sailing, a-trailing away.

Of all the wind upon the seas,
  A-sailing, a-trailing;
The best is an evening mackerel breeze:
  A-sailing and trailing away.

"A mackerel is a sailor-dish,"
Said Jones, "for 'tis a sailor fish,
All drest, like us, in white and blue,

Which I do call the prettiest hue
Which the great heaven has to show
Of all the colours in the bow:
So, if you please, I'll sing to you
A little song about the Blue!"

TRUE BLUE

BLUE is the sea we sail on,
And blue is the sky above,
        And blue are the eyes
        As sea or skies
Of the maiden whom I love:
And blue is the flag we're under,
And blue is the coat I wear;
        But brighter the blue,
        And deeper the hue

In the eyes which I hold so dear!
Bluer and brighter and sweeter,
Fonder and fair and as true;
Oh it's blue love and true love for ever!
And God bless the beautiful blue!

Now supper being over, every man
Lighted his pipe or called for a cigar,
Lolled in his chair—and all again began
To order "something lively" from the bar.
Jack Saltonstall, intent on keeping peace,
Waved a great South Sea club, and said, "I'm sent
By Providence to act as your police;"
And at the table sat as President.
He was a man of pleasing dignity,
And all allowed he would a captain be,
Calming all quarrels with a word and wink;
He had hot rum and lemon for his drink.
And as he sat in state, with the club of peace
Which he had taken from the chimney-piece,

He said to us: "What tales this bat could tell
Of many a battle—many a busted shell,
And murdered victims by the surfy shore,
And cani-bally feasts when all was o'er!"

Quoth Sam of Jersey, "I hev seen such things
Among them natives, ordered by their kings,
As well might make a common pirate weep,
And the old devil feel uncommon cheap:
Such derned, infernal deeds, and parst all showin',
Pirates and slavers ain't the worst folk goin'.
There's things to which the worst *they* do is slow;
I've lived among 'em an I ort to know.
And yet among those natives there are some
As mild as lambs, and good and humoursome;
Who never fight no more than an old hen,
Such difference there is in mortal men.
I'll tell you now a tale, to make you sport,
Of one who chanced among this gentle sort.

THE STORY OF SAMUEL JACKSON

I'LL tell you of a sailor now, a tale that can't be beat,
His name was Samuel Jackson, and his height was seven feet;
And how this man was shipwrecked in the far Pacific Isles,
And of the heathen natives with their suppositious[1] wiles.

Now when the others cut the ship, because she was a wreck,
They left this Samuel Jackson there, a-standin' on the deck—
That is, a standin' on the deck, while sittin' on the boom;
They wouldn't let him in the boat 'cos he took up too much room.

When up there came a tilted wave, and like a horse it romped,
It fell like mountains on the boat, and so the boat was swamped;

[1] *Vide* Appendix.

And of those selfish mariners full every one was drowned,
While Samuel, standing on the deck, beheld it safe and sound.

Now when the sea grew soft and still, and all the gale was o'er,
Sam Jackson made himself a raft, and paddled safe ashore.
For fear of fatal accidents—not knowin' what might come,
He took a gun and matches, with a prudent cask of rum.

Now this island where he landed proved as merry as a fife,
For its indigents had ne'er beheld a white man in their life;
Such incidents as rum and guns they never yet had seen,
And likewise, in religion, they were awful jolly green.

But they had a dim tradition, from their ancestors, in course,
Which they had somehow derived from a very ancient source:
How that a god would come to them, and set the island right;
And how he should be orful tall, and likewise pearly white.

Now when they saw this Samuel approachin' on his raft,
The news through all the island shades was quickly telegrapht,
How all their tribulations would speedily be past,
'Cos the long-expected sucker was invadin' 'em at last.

Now when Sam Jackson stept ashore, as modest as you please,
Nine thousand bloomin' savages received him on their knees;
He looked around in wonderment, regardin' it as odd,
Not bein' much accustomed to be worshipped as a god.

But he twigged the situation, and with a pleasin' smile
Stretched out his hands, a-blessin' all the natives of the isle;
He did it well, although his paws were bigger than a pan,
Because he was habitual a most politeful man.

So to return their manners, and nary-wise for fun,
He raised himself with dignity, and then fired off his gun:
So all allowed that he must be one of the heavenly chaps,
Since he went about with lightning and dispensed with thunderclaps.

They took him on their shoulders, and he let it go for good,
And went into their city in the which a temple stood,
And sot him on the altar, and made him their salams,
And brought him pleasant coco-nuts, with chickens, po and yams.

And from that day henceforward, in a captivating style,
He relegated, as he pleased, the natives of that isle;
And when an unbeliever rose—as now and then were some,
He cured their irreligion with a little taste of rum.

He settled all their business, and he did it very well,
So everything went booming like a blessed wedding bell;
Eleven lovely feminines attended to his wants,
And a guard of honour followed him to all his usual haunts.

Now what mortal men are made of, that they can't put up with bliss,
I do not know, but this I know, that Sam got tired of this;
He wished that he was far away, again aboard a ship,
And all he thought of—night and day—was givin' 'em the slip.

And so one night when all was still and every soul asleep,
He got into a good canoe and paddled o'er the deep,
But oh the row the natives made, when early in the morn
They came to worship Samuel, and found their god was gone!

Then Samuel travelled many days, but had the luck at last
To meet a brig from Boston where he shipped before the mast;
And he gave it as his sentiments, and no one thought it odd,
He was better off as sailor than when sailing as a god.

Now many years had flown away when Samuel was forgot,
There came a ship for pearl shell unto that lonely spot;
They went into the temple, and what do you suppose
They found the natives worshipping—a suit of Samuel's clothes!

And this was the tradition of the people of the soil,
How once a great divinity had ruled upon their isle;
Four fathom tall, with eyes like fire, and such was their believin',
One night he got upon the moon—and sailed away to Heaven!

"Wall, it's a fact," cried Doolittle, "I'll swear
A rover ain't contented anywhere;
But if he is a real sailor slip,
He's happiest on the hull—aboard a ship—
For there at times he has his tallest fun,
Especially if 'tis a dandy one
Where all is fine—O mateys, that's the thing!"
He raised his voice, and thus began to sing:
(While up and down he merrily did prance)
Unto the air of *Dance, the Boatman, dance!*

THE DANDY SHIP

WE'VE a dandy ship
And a dandy crew;
A dandy mate
And a captain too;

A dandy doctor
Who's a dand' old sinner,
And a dandy darkey
To cook the dinner.

Chorus. It's dance, sailors, dance!
It's dance, the sailors, dance!
We'll dance all night till the broad daylight,
And then go to sea in the mornin'!

We've a dandy lot
Of passengers,
Who live on chicken
And sassengers;
A dandy steward
To steer their mess;
Likewise a dandy—
Stew—ard—ess!

Chorus. It's dance, the sailors, dance!
It's dance, the sailors, dance!
We'll dance all night till the broad daylight,
And then go to sea in the mornin'!

"Shiftin' and changin' it is understood,"
Said Abner Chapin, "never come to good."
"Yes," quoth the Stranger, "that is very true,
Who goes for many gets but very few;
Who travels zigzag makes full many a cross,
And rolling stones ne'er gather any moss;
The explanation of which word is funny:
In common Yiddish Hebrew, *moss* means money,
And stones are men—take Peter for a sample—
Excuse me, friends, I know of an example
Of a loose fish who changed about so long
He first became a byword, then a song,
Which I will sing you though it is distressin',
Not that you need it—as a moral lesson."

JACK OF ALL TRADES

In all trades I've been a meddler,
Chorus. Foolin' my life away:
I started life as a Yankee peddler,
Fiddlin' and foolin' away.

Didn't find the trade encouragin'
So I turned a Dey Street New York surgeon.

Next I'd a shopman for employer,
And then a Philadelphia lawyer.

After that I was a smuggler,
Then I travelled as a juggler.

Next I was a collector's dunner,
And after that an emigrant runner.

Then I laboured with some bakers,
Next, for a year, I joined the Shakers;

But they found me too defective,
So for a while I turned detective.

Then I tried my hand as teacher,
And next became a Blue Light preacher.

Then I was one of the ——'s editors,
But had to cut to dodge my creditors.

Faking oranges I tried next on,
Then for a while I dug as a sexton.

For seven trips I was a slaver,
Then, as a barber, I turned shaver.

After that I worked as pirate,
For all the naval sharps to fire at.

Then nigger minstrel, then a sorter,
Off an' on, shorthand reporter.

Then I took to readin' lectures,
And after that to paintin' pictures.

Next as drummer I did chaffer,
And then I worked as photográpher.

Then for a while I run a dairy,
And next I turned apothecāry.

Then stuck pla-cards as a billist,
And so became a patent pill-ist.

Finding all other trades deceiving,
For a time I took to thieving.

Now I'm a Pacific purser,
And don't think I can do any worser,
Foolin' my life away.

"Yes, that's the way," said Jones, "that some go squandrin',
Which minds me that we too must now be wand'rin':"
"And I," quoth Brown, "must be aboard and early;
But first of all I'm going to see my girley;
She'd blow a storm if I should fail to meet her:
She is, I vum, an awful breezy creeter,
A gale in petticoats, and one that's stinging;
I'll sing a song on that—to end our singing.
You've known the *girl-wind*, boys—I never doubt it;
And here's a ballad which is all about it:"

THE GIRL-WIND

A HURLY-BURLY, hurl-wind
Is hurrying o'er the waves;
Before it runs the Girl-wind
Fresh up from the Ocean caves.

She's the little puff who goes before
To tell of the blow that's coming,
She sounds like a hive when winter's o'er
And you hear the bees a-humming.

It's all very well when a young girl can
Come tripping along with laughter;
But not so nice when you see the old man
With a big stick coming after.
It's just the same with Everything
When pleasure runs before us,
You drink your wine and think it's fine :—
Then comes the tavern scoreus!

So we went forth upon our different ways—
And these were wide—to many a distant shore:
I to my home to put in form these lays,
And think upon this strange wild sailor-lore,
In which, to him who reads with generous heart,

As in a museum we seem to see
The strangest relics gathered far apart—
Rude, coarse, and rough, yet touched with poetry;
Like shells and gems and coins of olden time,
And worthless stones, all hardened in a mass,
Such as I've seen, fished from the ocean's slime,
Such are these men and melodies—alas!
They all are of an age half past away.
Where is the boatswain now?—who hears his call?
And where these sailing packets once so gay?
I to myself do seem traditional
And all my youth a legend—so to say—
Yet well or ill I've done the best I could
To make in truthful song a little show
Of quaint old tales, now little understood,
Of the North End of Boston—long ago.

LAYS OF THE LAND

THE RISE AND FALL OF GLORYVILLE

WHERE the rockiest Rocky Mountains interview the scornful skies,
And the sager kinds of sage-bush in the middle distance rise,
There the cultured eye descending from the dreamlike azure hill,
Lights in an æsthetic foreground on the town of Gloryville.

It was in the Middle Ages—'bout the end of Sixty-eight,
So I found the hoary legend written on an ancient slate—
That one Ezry Jenks prospecting, when he reached this blooming spot,
Thus uplifted to his pardner: "Glory! Moses, let us squat!"

Thus rebounded Moses Adams: "Glory was the foremost word
Which in the untrammelled silence of this wilderness was heard,
And I arnswer, dimly feelin' like a prophet, grand and slow,
'Glory kinder sounds like Money—up to glory let her go!'"

And this casual conversation in the year of Sixty-eight,
As if by an inspiration he recorded on a slate,
Which 'twas said in later ages—six weeks after—used to hang
As a curiositary in the principal shebang.

On the spot that very evening they perceived a beauteous gleam
From a grain of shining metal in a wild auriferous stream:
As their eyes remarked the symptom thus their tongues responsive spoke:
"In this undiscovered section there *is* pay-dirt, sure as smoke!"

Little boots or little shoes it to inform you how, like crows
To a carcase, folks came flying, and the town of Glory rose;
As in country schools the urchins cast each one a spittle-ball,
Till at last a monstrous paper fungus gathers on the wall.

'Long the road they built their cabins, in a vis-a-visual way,
As if each man to his neighbour kind of wished to have his say;
But 'twas also said that like two rows of teeth the houses grew,
Threatening uncommon danger to the stranger passing through.

Yes, for like the note of freedom sounded on Hibernia's harp,
Every person in the party was a most uncommon sharp;
And it got to be a saying that from such an ornery cuss
As a regular Gloryvillin—oh, good Law deliver us!

First of all the pay-dirt vanished or became uncommon rare,
Then they wandered more than ever to the Cross and from the Square,
For when all resources failed them nary copper did they mind,
For they had fine-answering Genius, which is never left behind.

So they got incopperated as a city fair and grand,
Spreading memoirs of their splendour over many a distant land,
Mind I say in *distant* places—people near them knew
Into what unearthly beauty the great town of Glory grew.

Then they sent an ex-tra Governor over seas and far beyond,
Even unto distant Holland, loaded up with many a bond,
Splendidly engraved in London, having just the proper touch
Quite imposing—rather—for they did impose upon the Dutch.

And with every bond the Governor had a picture to bestow
Of the town of Gloryville a-bathing in the sunset's glow;
This they had performed in Paris by an artist full of cheek,
Who was told to draw a city *comme il faut dans l'Amérique.*

The ideas of this artist were idead from long ago,
Out of scenery in an opera, "Cortez in the Mexico."
Therefore all his work expanded with expensive fallacies:
Castles, towered walls, pavilions, real-estately palaces.

In the foreground lofty palm-trees, as if full of soaring love,
Bore up coco-nuts and monkeys to the smiling heaven above;
Jet-black Indian chieftains, at their feet too lovely girls were sighin,
With an elephant beyond them—here and there a casual lion.

You have seen in *Pilgrim's Progress* the Celestial City stand
Like a hub in half a cart-wheel raying light o'er all the land.
Well, in *that*, it is the felloes of the wheel which cause the blaze;
So in Gloryville the fellows were the ones who made the rays.

When these views were well matured the Governor went to Amsterdam,
Where to Mynheer Schmuel Ganef first of all he made his slam :
At a glance each "saw" the other—at a glance they went aside,
And without a word of bother soon the plan was cut and dried.

For one hundred thousand dollars then the Governor at will
Gave away the full fee-simple of the town of Gloryville.
"Dat for you," said Schmuel Ganef, "is, I dink, not much too much,
But I makesh de shtock a million ven I sells him to the Dutch."

And the secret of his selling was upon the artful plan
Known to the police in Paris as the *vol Américain*,
Whereby he who does the spilling manages the man who's spilt
Very nicely, for he makes him an accomplice in the guilt.

Even as of old great sages managed the Parisian *fonds*,
So in Amsterdam Heer Ganef peddled out his Glory bonds;
And to all he slyly whispered, "I will let you in de first
On de ground-floor—sell out quickly—for you know de ding may burst."

Woe to you who live by thieving, though you be of rogues the chief,
Even the greatest will discover in due time his master-thief.
True, he "let them in," and truly on the very bottom floor,
But was with the Gloryvillins in the cellar long before.

And to tell you how the biters all got bitten were in vain;
Here the Governor leaves my story, and he comes not in again.
I will pass to later ages, when all Gloryville, you bet,
Found itself extreme encumbered with an extra booming debt.

Those who sold the bonds had vanished, those who hadn't held the town,
Little knew they of its glory over seas or great renown.
They had nothing of the fruitage, though, alas! they held the plant,
Nothing saw they of the picture, save, indeed, the Elephant.

He who had been in the background now came trampling to the fore;
Terribly he trampled on them, very awful was his roar!
Very dreadful is the silence when no human voice responds
To a legal requisition for the interest of our bonds.

But ere long a shrewd reflection unto Moses Adams came—
"Darned ef I'm a-gwine to suffer fur another party's game;
Wings is given to muskeeters—like muskeeters men can fly;
Ef a strawberry-vine can travel with its roots, then why not I?"

Silently, in secret, Moses to himself a plan reveals,
Got a three-inch plank and sawed it into surreptitious wheels,
And when night in solemn mystery had succeeded unto day,
Put his hut and things on axles, and quite lonely drove away

To a place just over yonder by the old Coyote Road;
There, no more a man of glory, Moses Adams dropped his load,
And when resting from his labour and refreshing from his jug,
Having known a town called Julesberg, called his shanty Splendourbug.

On the following morn as usual in due time arose the sun,
And the Gloryvillins followed his example one by one;
While he smiled upon the city, as on other things beneath,
'Twas observed one snag was wanting in the double row of teeth.

Little said the Left-behinders, but they seemed to take the hint,
And each man surveyed his neighbour with a shrewd and genial squint;
All day long there was a sound of sawing timber up and down,
Seven more houses in the morning were a-wanting in the town.

And before the week departed all the town departed too,
Just like the swallows in the autumn to another soil they flew;
Only that, unlike the swallows which we hear of in the song,
When the Gloryvillins squandered each one took his nest along.

All except one ancient darkey, obstinate and blind and lame,
Who for want of wheels and credit could not follow up the game;
So the others had to leave him, which they did without regret,
Left him there without a copper—just one million deep in debt.

If you seek them you may find them comfortable as in a rug,
All of them at length established in the town of Splendourbug;
And the driver to the traveller as by Gloryville he goes,
Points him out, an ancient darkey who a million dollars owes.

IN THE WRONG BOX

WHEN Eagle Davis died,
I was sittin' by his side,
'Twas in Boston, Massachusetts; and he said to me, "Old boy!
This climate—as you see—
Isn't quite the size for me;
Dead or livin', take me back if you can to Ellanoy!"

So I took him by the hand,
But he'd just run out his sand,
And his breath was gone for ever—before a word would come;
Then I and other three
Together did agree
In a party for to travel and to funeralise him home.

But Goshen Wheeler said,
As he looked upon the dead,
Weepin' mildly, "Just remark my observation what I say:
That deceased, now glori*ous*,
Was in life a curious cuss,
And somethin' unexpectable will happen on the way.

"Frum the time that he was born
Till he doubled round the Horn
Of Death, all his measurements and pleasurements were odd;
And odd his line will be,
As you're registered to see,
Till his walnut case is underneath the gravel and the sod."

It was bitter winter weather
When we all four got together
At the depôt with the coffin in an extra packin' box;
And a friend with good intent,
A cask of whisky sent,
Just to keep our boats from wrackin', as they say, upon the rocks.

Then a ticket agent he
Seein' mournin', says to me,
"Can I get the cards, or help you in your trouble, Mister Brown?"
So with solemn words I said,
As I pinted to the dead,
"There you'll find, I guess, our pilgrimage and shrine is written down."

Then all night beneath the stars
We sat grimly in the cars,
Sometimes sleepin', sometimes thinkin', sometimes drinkin', till the dawn;
And each man went in his turn
To the baggage-crate to learn
If the box was keepin' time with us, and how 'twas gettin' on.

Then all day beneath the sun
Still the train went rushin' on,
While we still kep' as silent as grave-stones as we went:
Playing euchre solemnly,
Which we kinder did agree
With the stakes to build for Davis a decent monu*ment.*

'Bout once in every mile
Some mourner took a smile,
But we did no other smilin' as we travelled day or night ;
And once in every hour
Some one went into the bower,
And reported the receptacle of Davis was all right.

But when four days were past,
Which we still were flyin' fast,
Goshen Wheeler, very solemn, with expression to us cries,
"Where we are it should be freezin'
And our very breaths a-squeezin',
Whereas the air is hot enough to bake persimmon pies.

"Don't you smell a rich perfume
As of summer flowers in bloom?
'Tis magnolias a-peddled by yon humble coloured boy:
Now, I never yet did know
That the sweet mag-no-li-o
Grew in winter in the latitude of Northern Ellanoy."

Then said Ebenezer Dotton,
"I behold a field of cotton,
And I wonder how in thunder such a veg'table got here.
I don't know how we're fixed,
But the climate's getting mixed,
And it's spilin' very rapidly with warmness as I fear."

Spoke Mister Aaron Bland,
"I perceive on yonder land
That sugar-cane is bloomin', correctly, all in rows,
And not to make allusions
To Republican delusions,
But the niggers air a-getting' all around as thick as crows."

Still we sat there mighty glum
Till along a fellow come.
And I says, says I, "Conductor, now tell us what it means,
Just inform us where we be?"
"Wall, now, gentlemen," said he,
"I reckon we air comin' to the spot called New Or-leéns!

So we rushed all in a row,
When we got to the depôt,
To the baggage-crate, a-wonderin' at these transformation scenes;
And we found out unexpected
That the box had been directed
Not unto Ellanoy, but to a man in New Or-leéns!

Without carin' if I'd catch it,
I straightway took a hatchet,
And busted off the cover without openin' my mouth;
And found a grand pianner
Which we'd followed for our banner
All the way from Massachusetts unto the sunny South!

Then I said, "I rather guess
I can see into this mess,
And explain the startlin' error which has given you such shocks.
When that Boston fellow, he
Asked the route I'd take of me,
I pinted, inadvertional, unto another box."

Now Eagle Davis lies
Beneath the Northern skies,
Where the snow is on the pine-tree while we are with the palm;
But I reckon if his spirit
Should ever come to hear it,
He'll be perfectly contented with the story in this psalm.

ZION JERSEY BOGGS

A LEGEND OF PHILADELPHIA

BEFORE the telegraphic wires
   Had ever run from pole to pole,
Or telegirls sent telegrams
   To cheer the weary waiting soul;
When all things went about as slow
   As terrapins could run on clogs,
      Was played a game
      By one whose name
   Was Mister Zion Jersey Boggs.

A Philadelphia newspaper
   Was printed then on Chestnut Street,

While 'crost the way, just opposite,
There lived a sufferin' rival sheet,
Whose editors could get no news,
Which made 'em cross as starvin' hogs;
The first, I guess,
Had an express
Which kind o' b'longed to Mister Boggs.

But in those days the only news
Which reëly opened readers' eyes,
Was of the New York lottery,
And who by luck had got a prize.
All other news, for all they cared,
Might travel to the orful dogs;
And this they got
All piping hot—
Though surreptitiously—from Boggs.

For of the crew no party knew
That Boggs did any horses own.

All sportin' amputations he
  Did most concussively disown;
For he had serious subtle aims,
  His wheels were full of secret cogs,—
    Well oiled and slow,
    Yet sure to go,
  Was Mister Zion Jersey Boggs.

One mornin' he, mysteriously,
  An' smilin' quite ironical,
Spoke to the other editor,
  The man who run the *Chronicle*:
"The *Ledger* has a hoss express
  By which your lottery news he flogs."
    "Yes, that is true,
    But what's to do?"
  Replied the man to Mister Boggs.

Then Mister Boggs let down his brows,
  And with a long deep knowing wink,

Said, "Hosses travel mighty fast,
But ther air faster things, I think;
An' kerrier-pidgings, as you know,
Kin find their way thro' storm and fogs:
Them air the bugs
To fly like slugs!"
Said Mister Zion Jersey Boggs.

"And in my glorious natyve land,
Which lies acrost the Delaware,
I hev a lot upon the spot,—
Just twenty dollars fur a pair.
These gentle insects air the things
To make the *Ledger* squeal like hogs;
That is the game
To hit 'em lame!"
Said Mister Zion Jersey Boggs.

The editor looked back again,
And saw him better on his wink.

"It is the crisis of our fate—
  Say, Boggs, what is your style of drink?
Step to the bar of Congress Hall;—
  We'll try your poultry on, by Gogs!
    An' let 'em fly
    Tarnation high!"
  "Amen!" said Zion Jersey Boggs.

The pidgins came, the pidgins flew,
  They lit upon the lofty wall;
They made their five an' ninety miles
  In just about no time at all.
Compared to them, the *Ledger* team
  Went just as slow as haulin' logs.
    But all was mum,
    Shut close an' dum,
  By the request of Mister Boggs.

Then on the follerin' Monday he,
  Lookin' profounder as he prowled,

This son of sin an' mystery,
Into the *Ledger* orfice owled.
"An' oh! to think," he sadly groaned,
"That earth should bear setch skalliwogs!
Setch all-fired snakes,
And no mistakes!"
Said Mister Zion Jersey Boggs.

"Why, what is up?" asked Mr. Swain;
"It seems you've had some awful shoves."
"The *Chronicle*," his agent cried,
"Has went an' bin an' bought some doves!
Them traitors, wretches, swindlers, cheats,
Hev smashed us up like polywogs.
They've knocked, I guess,
Our hoss express
Higher than any kite," said Boggs.

"Have you no plan?" asked Mister Swain,
"To keep the fellows off our walks?"

"I *hev*," said Boggs, as grim as death;
"What do you think of pidging-horks?
For in my glorious natyve land,
Acrost the river, 'mong the frogs,
I hev a lot
All sharply sot
To eat them pidgings up," said Boggs.

"They are the chosen birds of wrath,
They fly like arrers through the air,
Or angels sent by orful Death—
Jist fifty dollars fur a pair;
An' cheap to keep, because, you see,
Upon the enemy they progs."
"Well, try it on,
And now begone!"
Said Mister Swain to Mister Boggs.

The autumn morn was bright and fair,
Fresh as a rose with recent rain.

The pidgins tortled through the air,
   But nary one came home again.
Some feathers dropped in Chestnut Street,
   Some bills and claws among the logs:
         Wipin' a tear,
         "I greatly fear
   That all's not right," said Mr. Boggs.

Into the *Chronicle* he went,
   Twice as mysterious as before,
"And *hev* you heard the orful news?"
   He whispered as he shet the door.
"Oh, I hev come to tell a tale
   Of crime, which all creation flogs,
         Of wretchery
         And treachery
   That bangs tarnation sin," said Boggs.

"Them *Ledger* fellers with their tricks,
   Hev slopped clean over crime's dark cup.

They've bin an' bought some pidging-horks,
  And they hev *et* our pidgings up.
Oh, whut is life wuth livin' fur
  When editors behave like hogs?
    An' ragin' crime
    Makes double time;
  Oh, darn setch villany!" cried Boggs.

"But hark! bee-hold, to-morrer, thou
  In deep revenge may dry your tears;
I hev a plan, which, you'll allow,
  Beats all-git-out when it eppears.
The ragin' eagle of the North,
  The bird which all creation flogs,
    Will cause them horks
    To walk ther chalks,
  An' give us grand revenge," said Boggs.

'Them glorious birds of liberty,
  Them symbols of our country's fame,

Wild, sarsy, furious, and free,
   Indeliably rowdy game;
They shall revenge them gentile doves,
   Our harmless messengers, by Gogs!
         In which the horks
         Hev stuck ther forks,"
   Cried Mister Zion Jersey Boggs.

"For in my glorious natyve land
   Acrost the river, down below,
I hev a farm, and in the barn
   Six captyve eagles in a row:
One hundred dollars fur a pair;
   Fetch out the flimsies frum your togs
         An' up on high
         I'll make 'em fly,"
   Said Mister Zion Jersey Boggs.

But this same editor had heard
   Some hint or rumour, faint or dim,

How Mister Boggs, it was averred,
Was coming Paddy over him.
An earlier tale of soapy deeds
Then gave his memory startling jogs,
And full of wrath
Right in his path
He went for Zion Jersey Boggs.

"Horses and pidgins—pidgin-horks"—
That was enough to raise his Dutch:
He saw it all—and also saw
The eagle—"Just one bird too much."
Too mad to mind his shootin'-iron,
And throw good powder to the dogs,
He grabbed his chair,
And then and there
Corrected Zion Jersey Boggs.

After long years had rolled away,
And Morse's telegraph came in,

Still on the facing rival roofs
  Two grey old cages could be seen,
And young reporters o'er their drinks
  Would tell each other—jolly dogs—
    Of ancient time
    What in this rhyme
  I've told of Zion Jersey Boggs.

THE BALLAD OF THE GREEN OLD MAN

It was a balmeous day in May, when spring was springing high
And all amid the buttercups the bees did butterfly;
While the butterflies were being enraptured in the flowers,
And winsome frogs were singing soft morals to the showers.

Green were the emerald grasses which grew upon the plain,
And green too were the verdant boughs which rippled in the rain,
Far green likewise the apple hue which clad the distant hill,
But at the station sat a man who looked far greener still.

An ancient man, a boy-like man, a person mild and meek,
A being who had little tongue, and nary bit of cheek.
And while upon him pleasant-like I saw the ladies look,
He sat a-counting money in a brownsome pocket-book.

Then to him a policeman spoke: "Unless you feel too proud,
You'd better stow away that cash while you're in this here crowd;
There's many a chap about this spot who'd clean you out like ten."
"And can it be," exclaimed the man, "there are such wicked men?

"Then I will put my greenbacks up all in my pocket-book,
And keep it buttoned very tight, and at the button look."
He said it with a simple tone, and gave a simple smile—
You never saw a half-grown shad one-half so void of guile.

And the bumble-bees kept bumbling away among the flowers,
While distant frogs were frogging amid the summer showers,
And the tree-toads were tree-toadying in accents sharp or flat—
All nature seemed a-naturing as there the old man sat.

Then up and down the platform promiscuous he strayed,
Amid the waiting passengers he took his lemonade,
A-making little kind remarks unto them all at sight,
Until he met two travellers who looked cosmopolite.

Now even as the old was green, this pair were darkly-brown;
They seemed to be of that degree which sports about the town.
Amid terrestrial mice, I ween, their destiny was Cat;
If ever men were gonoffs,[1] I should say these two were that.

And they had watched that old man well with interested look,
And gazed him counting greenbacks in that brownsome pocket-book;
And the elder softly warbled with benevolential phiz,
"Green peas has come to market, and the veg'tables is riz."

Yet still across the heavenly sky the clouds went clouding on,
The rush upon the gliding brook kept rushing all alone,
While the ducks upon the water were a-ducking just the same,
And every mortal human man kept on his little game.

And the old man to the strangers very affable let slip
How that zealousy policeman had given him the tip,
And how his cash was buttoned in his pocket dark and dim,
And how he guessed no man alive on earth could gammon him.

[1] *Gonoff*, a Scriptural term for a Member of the Legislature, or suchlike.

In ardent conversation ere long the three were steeped,
And in that good man's confidence the younger party deeped.
The p'liceman, as he shadowed them, exclaimed in blooming rage,
"They're stuffin' of that duck, I guess, and leavin' out the sage."

He saw the game distinctly, and inspected how it took,
And watched the reappearance of that brownsome pocket-book,
And how that futile ancient, ere he buttoned up his coat,
Had interchanged, obliging-like, a greensome coloured note.

And how they parted tenderly, and how the happy twain
Went out into the Infinite by taking of the train;
Then up the blue policeman came, and said, "My ancient son,
Now you have gone and did it; say what you have been and done?"

And unto him the good old man replied with childish glee,
"They were as nice a two young men as I did ever see;
But they were in such misery their story made me cry;
So I lent 'em twenty dollars—which they'll pay me by-and-bye.

"But as I had no twenty, we also did arrange,
They got from me a fifty bill, and gimme thirty change;
But they will send that fifty back, and by to-morrow's train——"
"That note," out cried the constable, "you'll never see again."

"And that," exclaimed the sweet old man, "I hope I never may,
Because I do not care a cuss how far it keeps away;
For if I'm a judge of money, and I *reether* think I am,
The one I shoved was never worth a continental dam.

"They hev wandered with their sorrers into the sunny South,
They hev got uncommon swallows and an extry lot of mouth.
In the next train to the North'ard I expect to widely roam,
And if any come inquirin', jist say I ain't at home."

The p'liceman lifted up his glance unto the sunny skies,
I s'pose the light was fervent, for a tear were in his eyes,
And said, "If in your travels a hat store you should see,
Just buy yourself a beaver tile and charge that tile to me."

While the robins were a-robbing acrost the meadow gay,
And the pigeons still a-pigeoning among the gleam of May,
All out of doors kept out of doors as suchlike only can,
A-singing of an endless hymn about that good old man.

CARRYING COALS

In the gloomsome abysses where darkness is kept,
And the spirit of silence for ages has slept,
    In the great shaft of Pottsville, way down in the hole,
    There came seven parties, all dealers in coal;
But they never had been in that chasm before,
Nor had the sensation of darkness all o'er,
    Which so greatly expandeth the soul.

And one of 'em said, "It's an awful delight
To be infinite deep into no end of night,
    Where the heavenly sunshine can't manage to spring,—
    And, talking of that, I've a notion, by Jing!
Let we ourselves mine out some coal lumps to-day
To show to the folks,—which I think, by the way,
    Would be a poetical thing."

So they filled up their pockets, untried by a doubt,
And in the hotel they unveiled 'em all out;
    But their glances grew strange as they turned o'er the weight,
    Till one of them shouted, "By thunder, it's slate!"
Yet the youngest among them had dealered in coal,
And unto that traffic surrendered his soul,
    Since the Anno Eighteen Forty-eight.

For all of man's wisdom is only a dream,
Which passeth away like a plate of ice-cream,
    And the best of experience fails, as we mark,
    If you go for to dig when you're all in the dark;
For there's always a moral inside of a tale,
And big things in little things always prevail
    As sure as there's wood in the bark.

CAREY, OF CARSON

THE night-mist dim and darkling,
   As o'er the roads we pass,
Lies in the morning sparkling
   As dewdrops on the grass.
E'en so the deeds of darkness,
   Which come like midnight dews,
Appear as sparkling items
   Next morning in the news.

Away in Carson City,
   Far in the Silver Land,
There lives one Justice Carey,
   A man of head and hand;
And as upon his table
   The Judge a-smoking sat

There rowdied in a rougher
  Who wore a gallows hat.

He looked upon the Justice,
  But Justice did not budge
Until the younger warbled,
  "Say—don't you know me, Judge?"
"I think," said Carey meekly,
  "Your face full well I know,—
I sent you up for stealing
  A horse a year ago."

"Ay, that is just the hair-pin
  I am, and that's my line;
And here is twenty dollars
  I've brought to pay the fine."
"You owe no fine," said Carey,
  "Your punishment is o'er."
"Not yet," replied the rover;
  "I've come to have some more.

"Fust-rate assault and batt'ry
I'm goin' to commit,
And you're the mournful victim
That I intend to hit,
And give you such a scrampin'
As never was, nohow;
And so, to save the lawin',
I guess I'll settle now."

Up rose the Court in splendour;
"Young man, your start is fair,
Sail in, my son, sail over,
And we will call it square!
Go in upon your chances,—
Perhaps you may not miss;
I like to see young heroes
Ambitionin' like this."

The young one at the older
Went in with all his heft,

And, like a flyin' boulder,
At once let out his left;
The Court, in haste, ducked under
Its head uncommon spry,
Then lifted the intruder
With a puncher in the eye,—

A regular right-hander;
And like a cannon-ball,
The young man, when percussioned
Went over on the wall.
In just about a second,
The Court, with all its vim,
Like squash-vines o'er a meadow,
Went climbing over him.

Yea, as the pumpkin clambers
Above an Indian grave,
Or as the Mississippi
Inunders with its wave,

And merrily slops over
  A town in happy sport,
E'en so that man was clambered
  All over by the Court.

And in about a minute
  That party was so raw,
He would have seemed a stranger
  Unto his dearest squaw;
Till he was soft and tender,
  This morsel once so tough,
And then, in sad surrender,
  He moaned aloud, "Enough!"

He rose; and Justice Carey
  Said to him ere he went,
"I do not think the fightin'
  You did was worth a cent.
I charge for time two dollars,
  As lawyers should, 'tis plain;

The balance of the twenty
  I give you back again.

"I like to be obligin'
  To folks with all my powers,
So when you next want fightin'
  Don't come in office hours;
I only make my charges
  For what's in legal time,—
Drop in, my son, this evenin',
  And I'll not charge a dime."

The young man took the guerdon,
  As he had ta'en the scars;
Then took himself awayward
  To the 'Ginia City cars.
'Tis glorious when heroes
  Go in to right their wrongs;
But if you're only hair-pins,
  Oh, then beware of tongs!

JOSEPHI IN BENICIA

THERE was a man who spent his mortal life
A-prisoning until there came a war;
And with the war there came an enemy,
And with the enemy came dynamite,
And with the dynamite the engineers
Histed that prison-house, and with it all
That was therein. And when the man came down
And lay a-dying, round the chaplain lit,
And asked him "What of life?" and he replied,
"To me this life has been a blasted cell."
And so he died like any other man,
And thus it is things work among mankind.

The great Josephi—the piano lord—
When in the land of California

Was duly published for Benicia,
Yet never once put in; and then arose
Dame Rumour with a hundred thousand tongues,
And people said that he had bust his wires,
And had neuralgia in his sounding-board,
And the dyspepsia in his pedal joint,
And the stricnosis in his upper keys,—
Yet all was false, and I will tell you why.
The day before he was to have gone in
Unto his glory in Benicia,
There came a visitor whose sun-grilled face
And grand prize pumpkin air had all the style
Of a Maud Muller's father; and this man,
Being shown in, remarked, "I s'pose you air
Mister Joseephee?" To him in reply
The small piano-smasher nodded "Yes."
And thus the agriculturist went on:—
"I'm from Beneesh, I am, and I belong
To the Town Council—that is my posish.
Down here disposin' of my barley, and
I thort I'd call and see yer, being as

Yer comin' down ter-morrer fur to play."
"Ja, dot is so," replied the music man.
"Ye see, yer comin' to a stranger town,
And so I thort I'd let yer hev some pints
About the programme. We're a-payin' yer
A pot o' money, and of course yer want
To suit the ordience." "Vell, vot you like,"
Exclaimed the great musician. "I can blay
Chopin, Beethoven, Liszt—ja! all de crate
Gombosers, and I gifes you vot you shoose."
"I never heerd them tunes," replied his guest.
"Do yer know 'Nancy Lee'?" "Not I, bei Gott!"
"Nor 'Mary Ann'?" "Nein" (*very haughtily*).
"The 'Spanish Dona'—the 'Monastery Bells'?"
"Gott's dammerwetter! Himmelspotzen—NEIN!"
"Wall, now, whar did ye learn? My darter Sue
Goes to Miss Lynch's, and she knows 'em all,
An' plays 'em all by heart right straight along.
I never thought her no great shakes, and yet
She's clean ahead of you." A gloomy pause
Ensued, and two long glares. Then he set on,

"What kind o' dancing music are ye gwine
To fetch along? for that's the heavy jerk."
"*Tantz musik!*" Oh, the horror of the voice
Of great Josephi when he heard these words.
"Yes, certinly. Ain't ye a-goin' to play
Fur dancing arter supper? Wot d'ye s'pose
We're gwine to pay yer fur?" (Here came the squall.)
"Go to der Teufel mit your tantz musik!
Dere-to your tauter also. Sapperment!
Verflucht sei deine Seele—do you dink
I coom to blay fur caddle? I ton't go
Unto Benicia. Dell your veller-bigs
Your tauter blays in my blace—in de blace
Of Herr Josephi—do you oonderstand,
You hundert tousend plasted *Schweinigel!*"
And in the rustic's face he slammed the door.

He did not play in fair Benicia,
And in that town he is not popular;

And in its leading circles seven out
Of eight regard him as a German fraud,
Who cannot even play "My Mary Ann."
And thus it is they think he is a sell,
And thus it is things work among mankind.

THE STORY OF A LIE

Who asks an ape to throw a coco-nut
Should take it not amiss if it be thrown
On his own head, as echo answers song.

There was a man named Jesse, who was called
The greatest liar in Connecticut.
For there are giants among the Brobdingnags.

It was a burning day, and William Hoop
Sat in the shade, when Jess came riding by.
When wolves run past your door-step, let them run.

But William cried, "Stop for a moment, Jess,
And tell us a big lie." Jesse liked it not.
Ne'er ask a hangman how to tie a noose.

But hastily and sadly he replied,
"This is no time for lying now; oh, woe!"
A wanton widow may wear darkest weeds.

"Your Uncle Sol died very suddenly
An hour ago, and you would have me lie!"
Who weaveth nets is often caught in them.

"And I am riding for the coroner,
And for a coffin. William, learn from this
Never while living ask a man to lie."

Then William ran in and told his wife,
And he and she and all the family
Burst into tears. The thistle soon bears thorns.

And in his waggon, leaving everything,
They posted off and on, four miles away.
The eagle hastens at the eaglet's cry.

And when arrived they found the family
In the large kitchen, but in ne'er a grief.
It pains a man at times to miss his pain.

There Uncle Sol was buried—to the eyes,
In a great water-melon, lush and red.
Life's sweetest things are water after all :

Which rises in a mist, and comes again
As rainy tears. And William almost wept
For rage, because he had no cause to cry.

But after this he never did entreat
Another man to tell a lie to him.
Burnt child seeks not a second time the fire.

THE LEGEND OF SAINT ANTHONY

THE seek-no-further face of loveliness,
The perfect form of fawn-like springfulness,
Rich as a bonanza just unbound:
Catherine Van Peyster, of Fifth Avenue.

She lived a year in Europe—but for aye
In all the hearts of all who met her there;
And then her pa allowed her boundless cash,
Which she laid out in glorious works of art.

Such as the dream-like dresses made by Worth,
And heavenly hats by Virot, and all things
Refined, æsthetic, swell, and classical;
Yea, even a picture—she bought everything.

'Tis true it was a picture of herself,
And when she ordered it she simply said,
"I know that I am very beautiful,
My mirror tells me that—distinctively;

"But I am also very clever too,
For I am of a clever family,
Papa and sisters all are awful smart;
Now you must make it somehow sparkle out

"In what you paint. And as for me I guess
I'll show you how to fix it—wait a bit.
Ain't there a saint they call Saint Catherine?
One of my beaux, I think, once called me that."

"*Si, Illustrissima*," the artist said,
"Dere is a Santa Catarina, who
Is beautiful most of the oder sants,
Vitch giusto suit so lovely mad as you!

"And she do always hold opon a vheel."
"I see!" cried Miss Van Peyster—"just the thing,
The wheel of fortune—and the loveliest saint;
That's me exactly. What a perfect fit!"

And so 'twas painted, and the painted pair,
Saint Catherine and Miss Catherine, went across
Unto New York; and many people came
To call and worship—or to make believe.

And with the rest came Mr. Anthony,
A blooming broker, and a mighty man,
Who did not think small brewings of himself,
Albeit his studies had been very small,

And very few i' the heap. His face and form
Were greasiness and grossness well combined,
With sneeriness and nearness in the eyes;
He seemed a kind of coarsest Capuchin.

And much he did admire the quaint conceit
Of being taken as a holy saint,
And said, "I'd like to try that thing myself.
How could a feller fix it——Catherine?"

"Easy enough," replied the beautiful:
"You've only got to send your photograph
Out to my man in Florence, and to say,
'*Vous peignez moi comme le Saint Anthony.*'

"I'll write it for you if you have a card,
And he will fix it for you *comme il faut*."
That very hour the heavy shaver wrote,
And sent the order for his portraiture.

And in due time 'twas done—and further on
'Twas in the Custom House—and thence 'twas sent
To the Spring Exhibition in New York,
There was no time to send it to "the House."

And Anthony himself beheld it not
Till it had hung a week upon "the walls,"
And all the newspapers had served it up,
And all the world had merry made withal.

Yea, he *was* in it—clad in dirty rags,
A vile abomination. In his hand
A monstrous rosary. The Sunday Press
Said 'twas a rope of onions, meant to feed

The monstrous hog which filled the canvas up,
So vast in its proportions that it seemed
As Anthony were waiting on the hog,
And not the hog upon Saint Anthony.

In it and in for it. Just as the Saint
Of Padua is painted, with his pig,
Only a little more so. And thus ends
The tale of the great hog and Anthony.

A RUSSIAN LYRIC

AIR—"*Denkst du daran mein tapfre Lagienka.*"

"SALTOKOFF SKUPCHIROFSKY," said the ruler
Of Russia to his captain of the guard,
I will retire; the night is growing cooler
Have all the troops been posted in the yard?"
"They have, my liege, and in the tower o'er you
The watchman, with an opera-glass, afar
Looks out to see that no one comes to bore you:
Bogu Tsarachnie! God protect the Tsar!"

"What have you done with him who came this morning,
And wanted me to buy a lightning-rod?"
"He sleeps beneath the Neva, as a warning
To others like him, not as yet in quod."

"The girl who bored us for a contribution
To send her blessed clergyman afar?"
"She's strangled by the Seventh Resolution:
Bogu Tsarachnie! God protect the Tsar!"

"And where is he who gave us the conniptions,
That cheeky man from the United States,
"Who came unto my bedside for subscriptions
To—what was it?—the 'Life of Sergeant Bates'?"
"Upon a special train that man is flying
Unto Siberia in a third-class car;
Thou badest him 'dry up!' and he *is* drying:
Bogu Tsarachnie! God protect the Tsar!"

"And where is he who bored us for insurance
On life or fire, who down the chimney came?"
"My liege, beneath our feet in deepest durance
He pays with penance for his little game."
"And, after him, the pedlar who came plungin'
Into the parlour, smoking a cigar?"

"Ask of the vipers in the palace dungeon:
Bogu Tsarachnie! God protect the Tsar!"

"And that young man who always kept a-saying,
'That is the kind of hair-pin that I am'?"
"My liege, the strychnine in his vitals playing
May tell you how I stopped that kind of flam.
"And he who at this day is still repeating,
'What, never, never?'" "In a butt of tar
We coopered *him.* His heart's no longer beating:
Bogu Tsarachnie! God protect the Tsar!"

"And where is he who on the imperial fences
Inscribed *Pop's Bitters*, and *Take Fooler's Pills?*"
"My lord, his medicines were no defences,
In Hades he atones for earthly ills."
"And that confounded nuisance of a Scotch Guard
Who played the bagpipes up and down the car?"
"My lord, the imperial headsman wears his watch-guard:
Bogu Tsarachnie! God protect the Tsar!"

"Captain, 'tis well. Now telegraph to London
That every Nihilist has had his dose,
And that a fresh conspiracy is undone,
And keep the gum-drop, corn-ball peddlers close
Who spread sedition in the trains to 'stress me;
And keep the gates of anarchy ajar;
So may Saint Feoderskidobry bless thee!
Bogu Tsarachnie! God protect the Tsar!"

MELODRAMNATION

"Now Mr. Gallagher is satisfied."
So says the Boston *Post.* The facts are these:
He is the chief of a theatric club,
And as he deems that he can melodram,
He melodrammed for it a mighty piece
Of thundering incidents and awful scenes,
Which called for just nine actors. And they all
Declared that each had got the worst and curst
Of all the parts, and that 'twas written thus
To boom the fame of selfish Gallagher;
So the first night they came upon the boards,
With hearts like hornets and with souls like snakes
And feeling like old pizen, all agog
To be revenged upon the common foe,
Who was to act the hero. *Act the first:*

The hero and his mother meet to part,
And on her shoulders and o'er all her bust
The parent had put pins by papersful,
Till she was like a frightful porcupine;
And when she pressed her darling to her breast,
The pins *en masse* entered his very soul,
And pricked his nose, and ran into his cheeks,
So that he howled; but his mamma held on,
Easing her heart with rapturous revenge
While agonizing his. In the next act
He was on shipboard, and 'twas in the plot
That he should be knocked down and cuffed about
By a most cruel captain; and, God knows,
The captain played that part most perfectly,
Since in the start he went for Gallagher
With a belaying-pin, and laid him out
Secundum artem, and then let him up,
Only to let into him twice as hot,
'Mid rapturous hurrahs. In the next act
The hero led the crew to mutiny,
And Gallagher was glorious; but just then

Some one let down the trap on which he stood,
And there he was, up to his waist in stage,
Unable to get up or to go down,
And thus they kept him in captivity
While all the audience guyed him. When he strove
To climb they lowered him, and when he sought
To dodge beneath they highered him again;
So he went up and down like Erie stock
Until the scene was shifted. In the next
He fought the villain of the play, and this
Was Mr. Hencoop Smith, a stalwart rogue,
Extremely high on muscle, and the way
He lathered Gallagher about the stage
Was Awful Gardener. And when Smith should cry,
"Forgive me—I am crushed!" and Gallagher
Replied, "I'll have your life!" the hero lay
Under the table, while his adversary
Bemauled him with a chair-leg. It was o'er,
And Gallagher, all black and blue, went home
To plotter out revenge. On the next night
The piece was adverred to be played again,

And Gallagher sent round a messenger,
Who said he was too ill to play his part,
But he would send a substitute. He did—
A giant-like ferocious prize-fighter,
Under another name. And how he played!
He squeezed the mother into raving fits,
And jerked her wig away by accident,
And threw the cruel captain down the trap,
And larruped all the actors; and when Smith
Came on to fight, he took him by the heels
And mopped the stage with him until 'twas clean,
Then hurled him through the flat. All was a wreck:
And in the front seat sat the Gallagher
And laughed until he cried. Revenge is sweet!

A TALE OF IDAHO

When they had finished the ethnology,
And polished up the climate and the crops,
And glorified the different kinds of bugs,
And told in turn their lies about the snakes,
And fish and deer and things, of Idaho,
A pensive cuss in spectacles inquired,
"All this is well enough; now how about
Your educational facilities?
And let me see in dots the time they go."

"And that's the only thing we really lack,"
Replied the Ancient, with a silvery sigh;
"We do defect in *that* ostensibly.
We have the schools, but then we cannot git
The folks to run 'em, or who will remain

Adjacent to 'em, for they will not keep."
"How!—do they *die?*" "Wall, some on 'em expired,
Though Idaho ain't an expirin' State;
But I will tell you just the time they go.

"We had a fine young fellow from the East;
He licked the boys, and also kissed the gals,
And was all round uncommon popular,
Bein' likewise an awful fightin' man,
And there he *did* slop over. For one day
He met a grizzly bar upon the prowl,
And whistled to it, and the grizzly *come;*
But when he went he carried by express
All of that fine young man inside of him;
And that is just about the time they go.

"We had another from Connecticut:
A widder run him down, and married him
Inside the very school-house where he taught,
Just as an Injun cooks a terrapin

In its own shell, or as a lovely deer
Is sometimes aboriginally biled
Inside of its own skin, for that poor man
Has been in bilin' water ever sense:
They say she makes it solemn hot for him.
And that is just about the time they go.

"The third was well enough, but he was lame;
I needn't tell you how *that* one got spiled;
For sense he couldn't run, one day, of course,
The Injuns overtook him, and the way
They treated him was pretty nigh as bad
As if they had been widders, and that man
Their lawful spouse. They also made it hot,
Because they took and briled him at the stake.
And that is just about the time they go.

"Then we tried women-folks to keep the school.
We writ for one. She came; and as she lit
Down from the stage, a man proposed to her

And was accepted, and she married him
That very night; in fact, within an hour
He gin a party, and we had a dance;
But Education suffered all the same,
As she declined to teach, bein' inclined
To conjugate—excuse my little joke;
But that is just about the time they go.

"The second—wall, *I took* the second one
About the middle of the week she come;
But telegraphed unto the Institute,
'Send on some more; keep sending of 'em on.'
And so they kept a-comin', but they kep'
A-going speedier than they arrove,
For the third lady was abducted by
A highwayman before she got to us—
She took it awful kindly, I believe.
And that is just about the time they go."

"But why," exclaimed the wondering traveller,
"Don't you obtain a scareful, ugly one—

Some hideous old faggot, just like that
Tremendous terror with the lantern-jaws
By yonder ticket-window? She would keep."
"Alas! how strange," replied the Ancient Man;
"How is it that you people from the East
Will never understand us pioneers?
That woman is my wife—the very one
I cut away from school; and she's by far
The handsomest there was in all the drove.
For that is just about the time they go."

A CALIFORNIAN ROMANCE

KNOW'ST thou the burning lay of Dante's own,
"*Nix mangiare è il diavolo!*
Ma peggior la donna"? that's to say,
"'Tis hard to be hard up, but harder still
To get ahead of women." Never much,
While in Night's cushion stars like pin-heads shine.

Oh, listen to me, for the tale I tell
Is of Chicago, and the latest out,
And by the noble *Tribune* novelist.
"Say, do you mean it, honest Injun, now?"
Said Vivian O'Riley to his sire.
"And faith I do," the earnest sire replied:
"Marry this girl if so ye choose, me son,

But—if ye do—the divil a ha'penny
Of all me fortune will yees ever see,
While in Night's cushion stars like pin-hids shine."

Two hours have passed, and so have eight or ten
Slow-rolling tramway cars, until there comes
The one which Vivian wants, and soon it lands
The lover at the door of Pericles
O'Rourke, the father of *bellissima*,
The Lady Ethelberta. Lo, she sits
In her boudoir (the high-toned word for "room"),
Casting her soul in reverie o'er the trees,
While in Night's cushion stars like pin-heads shine.

"I have bad news for you, my utmost own,"
Said Vivian in sad tones unto his love.
"Cusses and crocuses upon my luck!
And damns and daffodils on everything!"
And as he spoke there came into his face

A grey old scaly look which seemed to say,
Don't bluff or you'll be called. "My dad and I
Have had a round about, and he has dis—
Sis—sis—inherited me; and I have
Been given the g.-b. on your account,
My be—b—beau—tiful. And I am now
A beg—egg—eggar for you, Bertie dear!
While in Night's cushion stars like pin-heads shine."

Her soft dusk eyes grew wide and serious.

"Yes," he continued, "I am regular poor,
Poor as a busted Indian, and of course
It follows in the logic of our life
That I must give you up. I cannot ask
One in the golden glory of events
To come and share a fate which runs upon
A thousand annual dollars. Ne'er a case.
While in Night's cushion stars like pin-heads shine."

She looked at him with an incarnadine,
Rich, passionate, scarlet-sanguine crimson flush
Surging into her cheeks. If it had been
A *full*, 'tis probable that Vivian
Would have gone under; but a *flush*
Could never scare him or his similar,
While in Night's cushion stars like pin-heads shine.

"Oh, Vivian!" she gurgled, like a dove,
"Oh, do you think I will let up on you?
And do you deem I would go back upon
The note I signed, and run to protest?—no—
Not while the snowy paper of my truth
Is quirèd by the young-eyed cherubim,
And in Night's cushion stars like pin-heads shine."

Three months or ninety days went by, and then
Upon a golden Californian
December afternoon, with azure skies

Like those of summer as they are produced
In less expensive countries, men beheld
A diamondaine wedding at the house
Of Ethelberta's sire. As Vivian
And his fair bride sat in the car—ri—age
Which bore them to the station, ever on
She gazed upon him like a Lamia
With a strange look, which one might call, in fact,
A weirdly precious smile. He gazed at her.
"And so you would not leave me, love?" he cooed,
"Even when you thought me poor?" And she replied,
"Never, my precious one. I learned lang syne
That when a sucker once drops off the hook
It never bites again. And well you know
That you were on the point of dropping off,
And so your pa and I put up the job
So as to land you, dear—as faith we did—
A little quicker. Oh, men, men, men, men!
If ye thus round, girls *will* get square with you,
While in Night's cushion stars like pin-heads shine."

THE STORY OF MR. SCROPER, ARCHITECT

Yes, I'll tell you how it happened—that, too, with all due respect
To the memory of Scroper, late departed architect—
How it came that he departed so abruptly in the train;
Why it was he's been so late, too, in returnin' back again.

Now some folks are born to greatness, some achieve it, as you've read;
And some justly stand and take it as it dollops on their head;
But in this sublime Republic, where it's help and help again,
We all generally make it in cahoot with other men.

Scroper was a fine young fellow, of a monstrous enterprise;
Likewise really ambitious, for he was so bound to rise,
And he left no stone unturned—nor a log—he rolled 'em all,
Till at last he got the contract for our new great City Hall.

Now, of all our mortal actors here upon this earthly stage,
The contractors have the hardest parts to play, I will engage;
Specially in bran-new cities, just between the knead and bake,
And where all the population are severely on the make.

What between the Common Council, and the more uncommon sort,
Politicians, Press, and preachers, Scroper fell uncommon short.
All of such as come a-plummin' when a puddin's to be had;
All against his best contractin' counteractin' mighty bad.

Therefore when this edificial had got up his edifice,
All who'd not been edifishing with him soon got up a hiss;
Said the stuff upon the buildin' was the worst that could be had,
Likewise called the architexture architechnically bad.

So it came one solemn evenin' in a Presbyterian rain
Mr. Scroper all in silence gently took the Northern train;
All he left was one small message to a friend who shared his home,—
When the darned affair blows over, telegraph for me to come.

So he sat one summer mornin', far away in Montreal,
Musin' on his recent patrons, while at heart he darned 'em all,
When there came a little letter datin' from his recent home,—
"*All the thing is quite blown over, back again we bid you come.*

"*For last night we had a tempest,—while the mighty thunder rang,*
Up there came a real guster, which blew down the whole shebang.
(*Shebang*'s a word from Hebrew, meanin' Seven, sayeth Krupp,
And applied to any shanty where they play at seven-up.)

"*Truly it was well blown over all to splinders in the night,*
And the winds of heaven are blowing o'er the ruins as I write."
Gentlemen, the story's over. It would last for many a day
If it told of every buildin' built upon the swindlin' lay.

THAT INTERESTIN' BOY

He sat upon the window-sill and jingled ninety cents. There came along another boy, who said, "How are you, Pence? You're goin' out a-Christmassin', I guess, among the Dutch, to buy some gifts." The other spoke: "No—not exactly much. I am in luck, this year, I am. I haven't any bills. My sister's sick, and can't expect no presents but her pills. My brother Ben's in Canada, away upon the wing. Of course, you know he can't suppose I'll buy him anything. My mother pulled my hair, last night, until she made me squall. Of course she knows that she's gone up for anything at all." "But there's your father," said his friend. "Well,—yes—I really thought that I was stuck on the old man, and that he had me caught, and I was kinder looking round to hunt him up a pipe; but then, this very mornin' he hit me such a wipe! That fixed his Christmas goose for him, and took away his joy. Now all this money's goin' to a good and clever boy, to buy him lots of pea-nuts and candy, I'll engage—with caramels; and that good boy is just my size and age."

MISS MILES, THE TELEGRAPH GIRL

Thy heart is like some icy lake,
  On whose cold brink I stand;
Oh, buckle on my spirit's skate,
  And take me by the hand!

And lead, thou living saint, the way
  To where the ice is thin,
That it may break beneath my feet,
  And let a lover in.

Spiritualistic Poetry.

SINCE Soul first basked in Passion's sun,
  I always ran to seed
In seeking One who'd gone and done
  Some great heroic deed;
And deemed I'd find Life's Earnest Truth
  In Gloriana Clarke,
Whose eyes were like two carriage lamps
  Advancing through the dark.

But as the rose of morning fades
   Before the fire of noon,
Or sparrows yield in sylvan glades
   To mocking-birds in June,
My Gloriana's stock went down—
   Its wheat all turned to chaff—
When I got in with Mary Miles,
   Who ran the telegraph.

Her brow betokened serious life;
   I knew my final queen;
A soul divine in gaiter-boots,
   A Dream in crinoline.
Her parasol a glory seemed
   Around a vivid saint,
The whole one spirit-photograph
   Illumed with heavenly paint.

And thus she lifted up her voice,
   That mission-mantled maid;

And thus she spoke with golden grace,
   And sacredly she said—
A-pointing at me all the time
   With that same parasol,
The light which gleams from silent lands
   Around her seemed to fall—

"You've told of great and holy deeds—
   I s'pose they all are true—
But in our telegraphic line
   We've some adventures, too;
And though I do not like to boast
   Of what I ever done,
One thing my Moral Consciousness
   Declares was Number One.

"Last Fall I was in Tennessee
   A-travelling might and main,
When all at once the engine broke—
   They couldn't run the train;

And if another train should come
'Twould rather make us scream."
List to the glorious deed she did,
This angel of my dream.

"I saw a telegraphic line
Was running by our *rout*,
Though not a house or a machine
Was anywhere about.
And the conductor said, said he,
With his wild eyes of light:
'Miss Miles, if we'd a battery,
I'd fix this scrape all right.

"'I'd send 'em down a telegram
Some twenty miles below,
And ask for help.' I looked at him—
'I'll fix the business, Joe.
Is there a pair of nippers here?
If so, those nippers bring;

And if you can't, a sharp-edged file
Would be a heaven-sent thing.' "

"Unshadowed girl! I see the dodge,"
I cried in rapturous joy;
"And didst thou climb the post thyself?"
Said she, "I did, my boy.
A higher law of moral truth
Gave courage to my soul;
I did not show my garters once
In going up the pole.

"No poet ever felt such thrills
In touching of his lyre
As I did when I found there came
A message through the wire.
That wire I cut, and 'tween my teeth
I held it—ay, with pride—
And with my tongue the current clicked
To the wire on t'other side.

"On one side came the message in
From some man in New York:
'*Buy if you can, at ninety-five,*
Five thousand sides of pork.'
And this same electricity
I changed as in a flash:
'*Send down an engine right away,*
Or we shall go to smash.'

"The engine came, and all were saved—
Yet life is but a Dream.
I live—thou livest in a cloud:
We are not what we seem.
Still craving for the Infinite
In Time's ideal lodge,
I grasped a truth—yet after all
'Twas but an earthly dodge."

I gazed upon that spirit grand,
Upon my knees I sank,

And from mine eyes the burning sand
  The scalding tear-drops drank.
Then soft she smiled: "If deeds like this
  Can yield such victory,
And I am in your line, my love,
  Then, love, I yield to thee."

Ho, maidens of Vienna's show!
  Ho, matrons of Lucerne!
Look out for us next summer, when
  We give your shop a turn.
I have won my soul's ideal,
  I have booked her for a wife;
And the Fancy and the Real
  Are united in my life.

AN AMERICAN COCK-TALE

PROFESSOR LUTHER CRANMER BANGS
Has travelled in Europe more than a year,
And no one need ever be troubled with pangs
At telling him aught which he thought was severe;
For there's ne'er a Yankee of any size,
No matter how sharply he chaffs or slangs,
That can boast he ever has taken a rise
On Professor Luther Cranmer Bangs.

He was the man whom Dr. Snayle
Read a lecture to on a morning call—
Read it clear through from bill to tail;
And Bangs like Old Piety bore it all.

Said Snayle, when the sheets were all up-read,
"I'm a-going with this to Boston, you know"—
"I'm glad to hear it," his listener said:
"I always *did* hate those Bostonians so!"

Well, last week on a City Atlas 'bus
The Professor and I went riding down,
While the driver politely gave to us
Opinions on things about the town.
And finding my friend was "prone to receive,"
And came from the Western land afar,
He told him just what one *ought* to believe
In politics, piety, love, and war.

Then glancing at Bangs, who sat to leeward,
Looking as mild as cambric tea,
He said: "I once 'ad—but I soon got cured
Of—a wish to go to Amerikee.
I was tired of always a-drivin' these cusses,
And so I thought I would like to range"——

"You were right," said Bangs. "In our Yankee 'busses
It's the *driver* who takes (and keeps) the change!"

Sharp glanced the driver at Bangs; then said,
"What scared me of goin' was this, d'ye see,—
I'd a friend in New York, whose letters I read;
And he wrote: In the whole of your country,
He 'ad looked the biggest graveyards through,
Looked 'em through with uncommon keer,
But never 'ad come to a single view
Of a cove[1] as wos aged fifty year.

"And as this is the case in hevery State,
I think there's nothink on hearth for cure'n
A chap hof a fancy to hemigrate
Like readin' of them graveyards of yourn.
So I thought I'd rather perlong my breath,
Tho' sometimes here a fellow they hangs"——

[1] *Cove*, a word erroneously supposed to be slang. It is derived from the Gypsy *covo* or *covi*, meaning *that*—that fellow, that thing.

'You are right, my friend. Choose your own way of death,
I go in for that," said Professor Bangs.

"But I see you have not understood
Why no aged person is ever found
Among us. We only want *young* blood
On our driving, thriving, Yankee ground.
Youth alone has the power to go it;
Old men are a drag on putting it through,
So we kill them off—and our tombstones show it—
Before they arrive at forty-two."

Here the driver gave a long *cher—rup!*
And gazed at the Yankee, dark and wan,
As if he had woke the wrong passenger up
While calmly Professor Bangs went on:
"In walking up and down Broadway,
Large mourning sign-boards at times appear
With this inscription in letters grey—
'*Elderly persons extinguished here.*'

"And they put in your hand a pamphlet small,
Adapted to people of different stations,
Which cites the law, and exhorts them all
To dismiss in peace their old relations.
'Why let them linger in a vale,'
It states, 'where often colds they catch?
Send them to *us*, and we'll end the tale
With politeness, humanity, and dispatch.

"'N.B.—For those who would die by the trigger
We've a merciful man who's a practised shot,
With an elegant room, and a careful nigger
To lay them genteelly out on the spot.
Our principal has a chemist of fame,
Whom he exclusively employs on
Those who set their checks on a different game
And like to pass to heaven by poison.'

"'Tis thus the ladies generally choose it;
They love to die without pain or pangs

By a nice little globule—who could refuse it?
None but a man," said Professor Bangs.
"A *saw buck* extra they always charge
For the stylish mode of extinguishing breath.
A saw buck's ten dollars. It's rather large,
But then it ensures you a *cocktail* death."

"Vot may that be?" said the driver, meekly,
In the tone of a greatly altered man.
I observed that he seemed to be growing weakly
Since the Professor his story began.
"A cocktail's a tipple—America vaunts of it—
So flavoured, so foamy, so spiced, and whirled,
That he who can get as much as he wants of it
Very soon drinks himself out of the world.

"'Tis said in the sky—right over Paris,
Where the American heaven is found,
Where everything brick-like and fast and rare is—
The cocks with tumblers for tails run round.

They cut to the bar for all things thinkable,—
All that is nice is a gratis boon,—
Then they come back with your favourite drinkable
And their sickle-feather's a silver spoon!

"But he who invented the cocktail brew is
The man before you. Thus came the hint:
I had once been kissing a pretty Jewess,
Who just before had been nibbling mint;
And in order to recall the taste
Which I found in pressing her luscious two lips,
I mingled brandy and mint, in haste,
With sugar and ice—and thus made Juleps.

"The first step was, therefore, the julep perfected,
Which gives us a *menthal* spirit of wine;
And finding myself thereby respected,
I sought to make bitter and sweet combine.
So I took of bitters aromatic
(I prefer the tincture of bark myself,

With orange flavoured, but if you lack it,
Try any kind on the bar-room shelf),

"And I fixed them with sugar, and ice, and spirits,
In a silver tumbler, lightning-quick, sir,
Which I shook till all their several merits
Were combined in one subtle and strange elixir.
Then I passed it through a silver sieve
Kept carefully free from spot or rust;
And the final jimglorious touch to give,
I threw in a sprinkle of nutmeg-dust.

"And I am told by the spirit-rappers
That in the American Paris-heaven,
Though they've fancy drinks which are total snappers,
There's nothing better than mine are given.
So they die in New York without any pangs,
For they know in the next world, to requite 'em,
They'll sit over Paris," said Mr. Bangs,
"A-drinking cocktails *ad infinitum.*"

Here we got down, and the driver said,
"Vell, *you*'re of the kind that will allers bang 'em!"
And turning our mocassins homeward, we sped
To that great American wigwam, the Langham.
Said Bangs, "O'er *my* eyes there is drawn no wool.
That man has no heart who would tell you a mock tale;
But story for story I told to the Bull,
What I call a real American cocktail."

JUDGE WYMAN

A RURAL YANKEE LEGEND

LONG ago, in the State of Maine,
   There lived a Judge—a good old soul,
Rather well up in "genial vein,"
   And not by any means "down on" the bowl.
N.B.—By "bowl" I mean the "cup,"
   And by "cup"—N.B.—I mean a *glass*,
Since neither bowls nor cups go up
   At present when we our liquor pass.
         (Although I recall—
         'Tis three years this Fall—
When travelling in the wilderness,
And things were all in an awful mess,
And our crockery, with a horrible crash,

Had gone its way to eternal smash
(It came, as the driver allowed, from racin'),
We drank champagne from a tin wash-basin.
Excuse the digression—*non est crimen*—
And return to our Judge, whose name was Wyman.
The Judge oft drank in a hostelrie
  Kept by a man whose name was Sterret,
Where he met with jolly company,
  But where the whisky was void of merit.
The real Minie rifle brand,
That at forty rods kills out of hand.

Well, it came to pass that one night the Judge
  At Sterret's, after a long, hot day,
Got so tight that he couldn't budge,
  And found himself "well over the bay,"
With a "snake in his boot" and one in his hat,
  Like a biled owl, or a monkey horned,
Tangle-legged, hawk-eyed, on a bat,
  Peepy, skewered, and slewed, and corned.

Couldn't tell a skunk from a pint of Cologne,
  Couldn't see the difference 'tween *fips* and cents;
And when he attempted to walk alone,
  Simply made a Virginia fence;
Till liquor yielded at last to sleep,
And he sank into Dream River—four miles deep.

Sanctus Ivus fuit Brito, advocatus sed non latro.
"Saint Ives the Briton first took a brief,
For though a lawyer he wasn't a thief."
This is what the story declares,
Which says he listens to lawyers' prayers.
Likely enough! perhaps he may—
Whenever a lawyer tries to pray!
But another legend, old and quaint,
Assigns them a different kind of saint,
With a singular foot and peculiar hue,
Whose breath is tinged with a beautiful blue;

  And this was *rather* the saint, I think,
Who inspired the young lawyers, twenty-four,

Who helped Judge Wyman to stow his drink,
And made them rejoice to hear him snore.
Who, save the devil, would not have wept
To see these graceless legal loons
Tricking the good old Judge as he slept,
And filling his pockets with Sterret's spoons?
With silver spoons; likewise for butter
A handsome ten-dollar silver knife;
Then put Judge Wyman on a shutter,
And carried him home to his loving wife.

If any ladies read these rhymes,
Which in Edgar A. Poetry are called "runes,"
They may just imagine what sort of times
Mrs. Wyman had when she found the spoons!
The Judge's grief was full of merit,
And his lady wasn't inclined to flout it;
But she quietly took the spoons to Sterret,
And nothing more was said about it.
A month went by, and *Fama*, the wench!
Had not spread a whisper to urge remorse,

And Judge Wyman sat on the legal bench,
    Trying a fellow for stealing a horse.
The evidence was all due north.
    It froze the prisoner every minute,
Till Judge Wyman called the culprit forth,
    And asked what "he had to say *agin* it?"

The prisoner looked at the planks of pine
    Of the little rural court-house ceiling,
At all the jury in a line,
    Then answered, his only small card dealing,
"Judge, I hev lots of honesty,
    But when I'm drunk I can't control it;
And as for this 'ere hoss—d'ye see?—
    I was drunk as blazes when I stole it."
Answered the Judge, "If this Court were a dunce,
    She would say, in law that is no excuse;
For the Court held that opinion *once*,
    But of late her connection's been gettin' loose.
One may be certain on law to-day,
    And find himself to-morrow dumb.—

But answer me one thing truly, and say
    Where'bouts it was you got your rum?"
"I drank because I was invited,
    And got my rum at Sterret's, d'ye see?"
"Mr. Sheriff," cried the Judge, excited,
    "This instant set that poor man free!
The liquor that Sterret sells, by thunder!
    Would make a man do anything,
And some time or other, I shouldn't wonder
    If it made a saint on the gallows swing;
It will run a man to perdition quicker
    Than it takes a fiddler to reel off tunes;
Why, this Court herself once got drunk on that liquor,
    And stole the whole of old Sterret's spoons!"

IN NEVADA

LIKE an awful alligator
Breathing fire and screeching hell-some,
With a pack of hounds behind him,
As if hunted by the devil,
Came the smoking locomotive,
Followed by the cars and tender,
Down among the mountain gorges,
Till it stopped before a village
As the starry night came on.

Just before a mountain village,
Where there was a howling shindy
Just around a bran-new gallows,
With a roaring blazing bonfire
Casting a red light upon it,

While a crowd of roughest rowdies
Shouted, "Cuss him! darn his vitals!
Bust him! sink him! burn him! skin him!
Evidently much excited
As the starry night came on.

On the gallows stood a culprit
Shrieking painfully for mercy.
As the train and engine halted,
Louder yelled the gasping victim.
Then out cried the grim conductor,
"What in thunder is the matter?
What's ye doin' with that feller?
Why've ye got both fire and gallows?"
And unto him some one answered,
As the starry night came on:—

"This all-fired, skunk-eyed villain,
Whom you see upon the gallows,

Lately stole the loveliest mewel[1]
That you ever sot your peeps on,
For a hundred shiny dollars,
Went and sold it to the Greasers;
But, as you perceive, we've nailed him,
And at present we're debatin'
Whether we had better hang him,
Or else roast him like an Injun,
Ere the starry night comes on.

"And I think ez ther ar' ladies
Here to grace this gay occasion,
In the train, and quite convenient,
We had better take and burn him.
'Twould be kinder interestin',
Or, as folks might say, romantic,
To behold an execution,
As we do 'em here in Hell Town,

[1] Mule.

In the real frontier fashion,
Ere the starry night comes on."

Up from all the assembled ladies,
And from all the passageros,
Went a scream of protestation,—
"What! for nothing but a mewel!
Only for a hundred dollars
Roast alive a fine young fellow!
Never, never, never, ne—ver!"
Falling on her knees, a damsel
Begged the maddened crowd to spare him,
And to her replied the spokesman,
As the starry night came on:—

"Since the lady begs it of us,
And as we ar' galiant fellers,
We will smash the tail of Jestis,
And will spare this orful miscrint,

Ef you'll raise a hundred dollars
To replace the vanished mewel.
Then this fiend, unwhipped, undamaged,
May go wanderin' to thunder,
Soon as he darnation pleases,
Ere the starry night comes on."

Straight among the pitying ladies,
And the other passageros,
Went the hat around in circle.
Dollars, quarters, halves, and greenbacks
Rained into it till the hundred
Was accomplished, and the ransom
Paid unto Judge Lynch in person,
Who received it very gracious,
And at once released the prisoner,
Sternly bidding him to squaddle,
Just as fast as he could make it,
Ere the starry night came on.

And the lady who by kneeling
Had destroyed the path of justice,
Seized upon the fine young fellow,
He who had the mulomania,
Or who was a kleptomuliac;
And she led him by the halter,
While the reckless population
Made atrocious puns upon it;
And she stowed him in the Pullman
As the safest sanctuary,
As the starry night came on.

It was over. Loud the whistle
Blew a signal of departure;
Still the dying bonfire flickering
Showed on high the ghastly gallows,
Seeming like some hungry monster
Disappointed of a victim,
Gasping as in fitful anger,
Pouring out unto the gallows

Or the sympathetic scaffold
All the story of its sorrow,
As the clouds passed o'er the moon-face,
And the starry night came on.

Soon the train and those within it
Reached and passed a second station,
And was speeding ever onward,
When at once a shriek came ringing—
'Twas an utterance from the lady
Who by tears had baffled justice;
Loud she cried, "Where is my hero?
Where, oh, where's the handsome prisoner?"
And the affable conductor
Searched the train from clue to ear-ring,
But they could not find the captive.
He had clearly just evaded
At the station just behind them,
As the starry night came on.

Then outspoke a man unnoted
Hitherto: "I heard the fellow
Say just now to the conductor,
Ere we reached the second teapot,
That he reckoned he must hook it
This here time a little sooner,
If he hoped to get his portion
Of the hundred, since the last time
He came awful nigh to lose it;
For it might be anted off all
'Fore he got a chance to strike it,
Ere the starry night came on."

And the Unknown thus continued:
"They hev hed that gallows standin'
All the summer, and the people
Mostly git ther livin' from it,
For they take ther turns in bein'
Mournful victims who hev stolen

Every one a lovely mewel;
And they always every evenin'
Hev the awful death-fire kindled,
And the ghastly captive ready.
It's the fourth time I hev seen it,
Comin' through and never missed it;
Only for a variation
Now and then they hire a nigger
For the people from New England,
As the starry night comes on.

"And they find that fire and gallows
Just as good as a bonanza,
For they got the Legislater
Lately to incopperate it;
And I hear the stock is risin'
Up like prairie smoke in autumn.
Yes, in this world men diskiver
Cur'ous ways to make a livin',
Ez you'll find when you hev tried it

For a year or so about here."
And the passengers in silence
Mused upon this new experience,
Most of all the fine young lady,
As the dragon darted onward,
And the starry night came on.

THE PHILANTHROPIC CLUB

I AM the member of a club of reg'lar noble seeds,
Whose object is to give rewards for philanthropic deeds.
We root for magnanimity as spiders hunt for flies,
So we lately held a meeting to award our annual prize.

Then our President reported with great solemnity
The case of Dayball Carter, a man in Tennessee,
Who plunged into a burning store as if his doom had come,
But emergéd with an infant—and a gallon jug of rum.

But the club could nowise settle, admitting all the fact,
If the baby or the liquor had inspired the noble act,
For 'twas proved he kept the liquor while he let the infant go,
So the case of Mr. Carter was adjourned *in dubio.*

Then the Secretary read us, in very moving tones,
The wondrous case of courage of General Pompey Jones,
Who found a hydrophobic dog upon a neighbour's farm,
And roped his neck and led him off where he could do no harm.

Then Brother Chunk, of Pewterville, declared that it was sad
To have to state that Jones had no idea the dog was mad,
And that in circles where he moved 'twas very freely said
He'd picked it up intending to come out one dog ahead.

Then the next case reported in the doings of the day
Was that of Huckleberry Pod, a man in Iowa,
Who slopped into a raging flood to save a drowning maid,
And did it like a beaver, as admiring neighbours said.

Then Brother Chunk again let down his fist with startling bump,
And said he'd found that Mr. Pod refused to make the jump
Till offered fifty dollars by the people of the town,
And that then he wouldn't do it till he got the money down.

Last of all we heard the instance of Golias Purple Fife,
Who went into an awful well to save a fellow's life,
A man who always spoke of Fife as of a blooming fool,
And who recently had done him blind in trading for a mule;

And on top of this, moreover, in addition, 'twas a fact,
He refused a quarter-dollar for this noble manly act,
And when they asked him what he'd drink, or if he'd take a bite,
He jumped in silence on his mule and rode into the night.

This case, in the opinion of the members of the club,
Was much the most deserving, and the nearest to the hub;
And each allowed he'd never heard the like in all his life,
So, by general acclamation, they bestowed the prize on Fife:—

A silver-plated snuff-box, with a compass in the lid,
With the words, "*If sold at auction always do as you are bid,*"
Which we sent him in a hurry ere it might be understood
That this, too, was not an instance of the pure unmingled good.

And these are the proceedings of these noble-minded seeds,
Who make it their profession to discover virtuous deeds;
And every day turns out a lot, but still 'tis on our mind
That a case without a speck in it is very hard to find.

THE COLOURED FORTUNE-HUNTER

PETE JONSING went to see the County Clerk
About a marriage license, and the man
Said unto him for fun, but seriously:
"I hope the bride possesses fifty cents,
Because the Legislature's passed a law
That any girl with less must not be wed."
"Jis' go ahead wid dat 'ar paper, Boss,"
Peter replied; then whispered, bending down:
"Dar's rumers—and dey is reliable—
Dat de young woman dat I'm goin' fur
Has got two dollars and a quarter—*shoa*.
And dat's de reason wy I marries her."

PENN

ON A TEXT BY ROBERT BURDETTE

When William Penn appeared before King Charles
To get the charter of his Promised Land
In Pennsylvaniá,
'Twas in his usual free-and-easy style,
With hands in pockets and his hat on side—
Singing *Lard-dardy day!*
Let us drink and be merry, laugh, sing, and rejoice,
With claret and sherry, theorbo and voice,
Merry-ton-ton-ton ta-lay!

King Charles at once removed his feathered tile.
"Keep on your hat, young man!" said William Penn,
"It is our Quaker way;

And people will not know that you are bald;
Be quite at home to make your guests at home—
Singing *Lard-dardy day!*
This changeable world to our joys is unjust,
All treasure's uncertain, so down with your dust,
Merry-ton-ton-ton ta-lay!"

"It is the custom here," the King replied,
"For only one to cover at a time;
This is the courtly way."
"Then you should have more covers," warbled Penn.
"Warm people's heads to make them merry men—
Singing *Lard-dardy day!*
And in frolics dispose of your shillings and pence,
Since we all shall be past it a hundred years hence,
Merry-ton-ton-ton ta-lay!

"'Tis a queer world, and faith! I do not lay
My hat around, loose, in a domicile
Where I don't know the way,

Unless some party gives a check for it;
I've travelled some—I have—and can't be bit—
Singing *Lard-dardy day!*
Since, despite your invention, and learning, and sense,
You'll be *non est inventus* a hundred years hence,
Merry-ton-ton-ton ta-lay!"

"Odds-fish!" exclaimed his Royal Majesty,
"He talks full well, but as it seems to me,
According to our way,
There's a tremendous pig in this same Penn."
"Bravo, young man!" said William; "try again—
Singing *Lard-dardy day!*
You have brought me a terrible one on the nob,
But I bear you no malice, not being a snob,
Merry-ton-ton-ton ta-lay!"

And thus it is that history is writ,
And thus it is good men are slandered sore
From ever till to-day.

Some writer pastes a joke; it may remain
Safe in a corner from Time's wind and rain
Till Time has rolled away.
So, hurrah for King Charles! and hurrah, too, for Penn!
And all such and similar excellent men!
Merry-ton-ton-ton ta-lay!

BALLAD OF THE FOXES

THERE is a golden glory in my song
As of a picture by Carpaccio,
For it is of the early morning-time
When every man believed with tender faith
That animals could talk—oh, lovely lore!
So, lady, listen as the lay runs on.

There was a goose, and she was travelling
Across the land for her dyspepsia,
And at the noontide sat to rest herself
In a small thicket, when there came along
Two starving foxes, perishing to find
Something which was not too-too-utter-ish

To serve for dinner. And as they were wild
For want of food, it was but natural
That they should likewise be confounded cross;
Oh, lady, listen as the lay runs on!

And as they halted near the thicket, one
Of them observed, "If you were half as sharp
As books make out, you would not now, I'll bet,
Be ravenous enough to gnaw the grass."
"And if you were as big, or half as big,
As you believe you are," snarled Number Two,
"You'd be a lion of the largest size
Minus his roar, and pluck, and dignity."
Oh, listen, lady, as the lay runs on!

"Please to observe I want no impudence
From any fifteen-nickel quadruped
Of your peculiar shape," snapped Number One.
"And if you give me but another note

Of your chin-music," snarled out Number Two,
"I'll make a wreck of you, you wretched beast,
Beyond insurance—bet your tail on that!"
Oh, lady, listen as the lay runs on!

"You are the champion snob of all the beasts!"
"And you the upper scum of all the frauds."
"You are the weathercock of infamy."
"And you the lightning-rod of falsehood's spire."
"You are a thief!" "Ditto." "You lie." "I ain't."
"Shut up, you goy!" And hearing this, the goose
Could bear no more, but walking from the bush,
Put on expression most benevolent,
And said, "Oh, gentlemen, for shame! for shame!
I'll settle this dispute: in the first place
Let me remark, as an impartial friend——"
Oh, listen, lady, as the lay runs on!

But she did not remark, because they made
A rush at her and caught her by the throat,

And ate her up; and as they picked their teeth
With toothpicks made of her last pin-feathers,
The first observed, and that quite affably,
"Only a goose would ever make attempt
To settle a dispute when foxes fight"—
Oh, lady, listen as the lay runs on!

"And while I have a very great respect
For any peacemaker," said Number Two,
"I would suggest that I invariably
Have found, if they be really honest folk
Who interfere with reprobates like us,
They're always eaten up; there is, I think,
More clanship between devils any day
Than among all the angels. Interest
Binds us together, and howe'er we fight
Among ourselves to ease our bitter blood,
We do not hate each other half as much
As we do hate the good. Neighbours who fight
Can generally take most perfect care,

Not only of themselves, but of the goose
Who sticks her bill into the fuss they make.
This banquet now adjourns until it meets
Another wingéd angel of the sort
Which it has just discussed—may it be soon!"
Lady, this lyric runs no further on.

EST MODUS IN REBUS

A NARRATIVE OF NEW YORK

I WOULD not say to man, "Don't spread yourself
To win the admiration of mankind,"
Since he who never spreads can never shine,
And he who never shines is never seen,
And he who's never seen is counted out
In the great game of life; yet what is spread
Too thin entirely, when the sun shines out
Must soon dry up and be a fly-away.

There was a man who took his daily dine
At a delightful *table d'hôte*, where he
Was waited on by an obedient youth,

Who, as a waiter, was a paragon
Of quick politeness. He'd apologise
If the sun shone too much, or if it rained,
And say in simple faith that he would speak
To the proprietor and have it changed,
Then vanish like an elfin fly-away.

The vulgar boarder at this *table d'hôte*
Was one who greatly loved to spread himself
And play the imperial before the rest;
And finding that the waiter cushioned it,
Sat down on him severely. Every time
He spoke he called him names, and said that he
Forthwith would punish him in cruel wise
Unless he tortled faster, or unless
The steak was better cooked. And then he'd swear—
Oh, death and dandelions! how he would swear!
Till all the blood of all the boarders round
Was almost turned to cherry-water ice,
And each and all wished they could fly away.

And yet this waiter had a fund reserved
Of pretty stout pugnacity and pride,
And every time the boarder called him "fool,"
Or "low-born rooster," he would add it up
To the preceding pile of expletives,
And think it over. He did not forget
A single word. Of all the abusatives
There was not one which proved a fly-away.

At last the crisis came, when one fine day,
For some imagined fault, the boarder said
Unto the waiter, that unless he stirred
A little quicker he would bung his eye,
And take him by the legs *instanter*-ly
And wipe the floor with him. But with that word
He overdrew the account. That was the fly
Which overset the camel, and the drop
Which made the pail slop over. For the youth
On that let out his Injun. All at once
He turned both red and white, as fat and lean

Are seen in a beefsteak before 'tis cooked,
And blew his soul out in a fly-away.

"You misspelled copy of a gentleman
With all the meaning lost!—if you dare call
Me names again as you have often done,
I'll bung your pallid eyes. You've said too much,
So now just dwindle down. I've always been
Obedient and polite, and served you well,
As you were never served by any one,
And all you ever gave me was abuse,
And all because you were a vulgar fool.
Now stop your noise, or I will sling you out
Of yonder window for a fly-away!"

The boarder rose as if in roaring wrath,
The waiter jerked his linen jacket off
And fairly danced about in gypsy style,
Impatient for a fight. But then the guest

As if with self-command restrained himself,
And said to the assembled company,
"There must be lines in all society
To regulate our conduct. Lines, I say,
Which separate us from the vulgar herd,
With whom we may not fight. I draw the line
At waiters." Here he looked about the room
To be applauded; but the only sound
Which rose was that of a tremendous slap
On his own face, and then a mighty roar
Of laughter from the happy company,
For all his valour was a fly-away.

So he sat down too terrified to speak;
And then the waiter took a dripping jug
Of ice-water and poured out every drop
Upon his head, yea, water, ice, and all;
And then that boarder burst in bitter tears,
And blubbered like a boy, while all the room
Rang with redoubled laughter. Then a guest

Proposed a vote of thanks to him who had
Put down a public nuisance, and the next
Passed round a hat and took collection up
To give the waiter as a small reward
For punishing a coward. Then he rose,
And since that hour has been a fly-away.

THE MASHER

The word to "mash," in the sense of causing love or attracting by a glance or fascinating look, came into ordinary slang from the American stage. Thus an actress was often fined for "mashing" or smiling at men in the audience. It was introduced by the well-known gypsy family of actors, C., among whom Romany was habitually spoken. The word "masher" or "mash" means in that tongue to allure, delude, or entice. It was doubtless much aided in its popularity by its quasi-identity with the English word. A girl could be called a masher as she could be called a man-killer, or killing. But there can be no doubt as to the gypsy origin of "mash" as used on the stage. I am indebted for this information to the late well-known *impresario* Palmer of New York, and I made a note of it years before the term had become at all popular.

It was in the Indian summer-time, when life is tender brown,
And people in the country talk of going into town,
When the nights are crisp and cooling, though the sun is warm by day,
In the home-like town of Glasgow, in the State of Iowa;

It was in the railroad deepô of that greatly-favoured zone,
That a young man met a stranger, who was still not all unknown,
For they had run-countered casual in riding in the car,
And the latter to the previous had offered a cigar.

Now as the primal gentleman was nominated Gale,
It follows that the secondary man was Mr. Dale;
This is called poetic justice when arrangements fit in time,
And Fate allows the titles to accommodate in rhyme.

And a lovely sense of autumn seemed to warble in the air;
Boys with baskets selling peaches were vibratin' everywhere,
While in the mellow distance folks were gettin' in their corn,
And the biggest yellow punkins ever seen since you were born.

Now a gradual sensation emotioned this our Gale,
That he'd seldom seen so fine a man for cheek as Mr. Dale;
Yet simultaneous he felt that he was all the while
The biggest dude and cock-a-hoop within a hundred mile.

For the usual expression of his quite enormous eyes
Was that of two ripe gooseberries who've been decreed a prize;
Like a goose apart from berries, too—though not removed from sauce—
He conversed on lovely Woman as if he were all her boss.

Till, in fact, he stated plainly that, between his face and cash,
There was not a lady living whom he was not sure to mash;
The wealthiest, the loveliest, of families sublime,
At just a single look from him must all give in in time.

Now when our Dale had got along so far upon the strain,
They saw a Dream of Loveliness descending from the train,
A proud and queenly beauty of a transcendental face,
With gloves unto her shoulders, and the most expensive lace.

All Baltimore and New Orleans seemed centered into one,
As if their stars of beauty had been fused into a sun;
But, oh! her frosty dignity expressed a kind of glow
Like sunshine when thermometers show thirty grades below.

But it flashed a gleam of shrewdness into the head of Gale,
And with aggravatin' humour he exclaimed to Mr. Dale,
"Since every girl's a cricket-ball and you're the only bat,
If you want to show you're champion, go in and mash on that.

"I will bet a thousand dollars, and plank them on the rub,
That if you try it thither, you will catch a lofty snub.
I don't mean but what a lady may reply to what you say,
But I bet you cannot win her into wedding in a day."

A singular emotion enveloped Mr. Dale;
One would say he seemed confuseled, for his countenance was pale:
At first there came an angry look, and when that look did get,
He larft a wild and hollow larf, and said, "I take the debt.

"The brave deserve the lovely—every woman may be won;
What men have fixed before us may by other men be done.
You will lose your thousand dollars. For the first time in my life
I have gazed upon a woman whom I wish to make my wife."

Like a terrier at a rabbit, with his hat upon his eyes
Mr. Dale, the awful masher, went head-longing at the prize,
Looking rather like a party simply bent to break the peace.
Mr. Gale, with smiles, expected just a yell for the police.

Oh ! what are women made of? Oh ! what can women be?
From Eves to Jersey Lilies what bewildering sights we see !
One listened on the instant to all the Serpent said;
The other paid attention right away to Floral Ned.

With a blow as with a hammer the intruder broke the ice,
And the proud and queenly beauty seemed to think it awful nice.
Mr. Gale, as he beheld it, with a trembling heart began
To realise he really was a most astonished man.

Shall I tell you how he wooed her? shall I tell you how he won?
How they had a hasty wedding ere the evening was done?
For when all things were considered, the fond couple thought it best—
Such things are not uncommon in the wild and rapid West.

Dale obtained the thousand dollars, and then vanished with the dream.
Gale stayed in town with sorrow, like a spoon behind the cream;
Till one morning in the paper he read, though not in rhymes,
How a certain blooming couple had been married fifty times !

How they wandered o'er the country; how the bridegroom used to bet
He would wed the girl that evening,—how he always pulled the debt;
How his eyes were large and greensome; how, in fact, to end the tale,
Their very latest victim was a fine young man named Gale.

ARIZONA JOHN

When in a situation it always pays the best
To have your wits about you, for it helps the interest;
And a man gets so encouraged by succeedin' when he tries,
That the more you crowd him downward, the more he's bound to rise.

As when near Tres Alamos, while workin' at his mine,
John Lyons, late of Tombstone, without the least design
To involve himself whatever in any kind of tricks,
Got inside an unprovided and a most unpleasant fix.

John Lyons, late of Tombstone, had but just put in a blast,
When he saw four buck Apaches approximatin' fast
Upon their headlong horses in a rackaloose career,
And every one preceded by a long projectin' spear:

He had planted all the powder, and was just atop the shaft,
While the foemen kept a-comin' like as they was telegrapht.
To run was to be taken, and to stay was to be slew—
And in such a situation how-whatever could he do?

Bein' quick upon the trigger Lyons did not stop to choose,
For a match was in his fingers, so he lighted up the fuse,
And dropped behind a boulder for to disabuse their aim,
When at him like a sheriff's writ full dig the Injuns came.

He had timed the fuse so nicely that the 'Paches reached the rock
Exactly at the nick of the explosionary shock:
Bang! How the big rock busted as the powder gave a flare!
While a rain of stones and gravel went a-thunderin' through the air.

It was four red Apaches who also had a rise,
And started for the hunting-grounds on horseback thro' the skies;
Or as if they had the notion, but recalled it there and then,
For they speedily descended as four non-existent men.

John Lyons, late of Tombstone, just down behind his rock,
Escaped the influential effect of such a shock,
And examinin' the prospect, he very plainly sees
He has worked the blast quite perfect—likewise slammed his enemies.

When narratin' the adventure which I've chanted in my song,
If he terms them "blasted Injuns" no one calls his language strong—
For their hopes were surely blasted which they fondly reckoned on,
And with patent giant-powder by this Arizona John.

THE BALLAD OF CHARITY

It was in a pleasant deepô, sequestered from the rain,
That many weary passengers were waitin' for the train;
Piles of quite expensive baggage, many a gorgeous portmantó,
Ivory-handled umberellas made a most touristic show.

Whereunto there came a person, very humble was his mien,
Who took an observation of the interestin' scene;
Closely scanned the umberellas, watched with joy the mighty trunks,
And observed that all the people were securin' Pullman bunks:

Who was followed shortly after by a most unhappy tramp,
Upon whose features poverty had jounced her iron stamp;
And to make a clear impression as bees sting you while they buzz,
She had hit him rather harder than she generally does.

For he was so awful ragged, and in parts so awful bare,
That the folks were quite repulsioned to behold him begging there;
And instead of drawing currency from out their pocket-books,
They drew themselves asunder with aversionary looks.

Sternly gazed the first newcomer on the unindulgent crowd,
Then in tones which pierced the deepô he solilicussed aloud:—
"I hev trevelled o'er this cont'nent from Quebec to Bogotáw,
But setch a set of scallawags as these I never saw.

"Ye are wealthy, ye are gifted, ye have house and lands and rent,
Yet unto a suff'rin' mortal ye will not donate a cent;
Ye expend your missionaries to the heathen and the Jew,
But there isn't any heathen that is half as small as you.

"Ye are lucky—ye hev cheque-books and deeposits in the bank,
And ye squanderate your money on the titled folks of rank;
The onyx and the sardonyx upon your garments shine,
An' ye drink at every dinner p'r'aps a dollar's wuth of wine.

"Ye are goin' for the summer to the islands by the sea,
Where it costs four dollars daily—setch is not for setch as me;
Iv'ry-handled umberellers do not come into my plan,
But I kin give a dollar to this suff'rin' fellow-man.

"Hand-bags made of Rooshy leather are not truly at my call,
Yet in the eyes of Mussy I am richer 'en you all,
For I kin give a dollar wher' you dare not stand a dime,
And never miss it nother, nor regret it ary time."

Sayin' this he drew a wallet from the inner of his vest,
And gave the tramp a daddy, which it was his level best;
Other people havin' heard him soon to charity inclined—
One giver soon makes twenty if you only get their wind.

The first who gave the dollar led the other one about,
And at every contribution he a-raised a joyful shout,
Exclaimin' how 'twas noble to relieviate distress,
And remarkin' that our duty is our present happiness.

Thirty dollars altogether were collected by the tramp,
When he bid 'em all good evenin' and went out into the damp,
And was followed briefly after by the one who made the speech,
And who showed by good example how to practise as to preach.

Which soon around the corner the couple quickly met,
And the tramp produced the specie for to liquidate his debt;
And the man who did the preachin' took his twenty of the sum,
Which you see that out of thirty left a tenner for the bum.

And the couple passed the summer at Bar Harbour with the rest,
Greatly changed in their appearance and most elegantly dressed.
Any fowl with change of feathers may a brilliant bird become:
Oh, how hard is life for many! oh, how sweet it is for some!

MULTUM IN PARVO

"GREAT thoughts are oft expressed in fewest words,"
And I remember how long years ago,
When a great lady in her diary
Of a short visit to the Scottish land,
Recorded of a sorrowful event,
"To-day poor little Vicky, by mischance,
Sat on a wasps' nest." All the newspapers
Declared it was a perfect masterpiece
Of excellent conciseness. Yet I think
It was outdone by a Red Indian—
One of the Quoddy tribe—who did the same;
Since he, like "little Vicky," also sat
Upon a seat as hot; and when he rose,
Briefly exclaimed in his vernacular :—

"*H'lam-kikqu'!*" and being asked what this
Might mean, responded in the English tongue:
"*Heap hell!*" O reader! if the soul of wit
Be brevity, this Indian was there.

THE ORGANIST OF BERGAMO

> " For blowing is not playing on the flute,
> To do that well you must put fingers to't."
>
> GERMAN PROVERB.

THIS is a Merry Tale of Bergamo.

It chanced in Fifteen Hundred Twenty-Eight
[As I do find the fact recorded in
A pleasing book of Sixteen Thirty-Six
Entitled *Scelta di Facetie*—
A little yellow, quaint, italic tome,
Which looks as if it were behind the age,
And would have been black letter if it could]
That in fair Venice raged a pestilence
Whereof in time full many people died,
And among these a trusty servitor
Who blew the bellows for the organist

All in the great Cathedral of Saint Mark,
Whose billowy pavement truly seems to roll
In time and measure with the music sweet,
So perfect were the harmonies of Art
Which men imagined in the olden time.

Now as this man had died while at his work,
Even while blowing a *Magnificat*
All in the holy church, it was adjudged
That he almost deserved to be a saint.
And he who preached the sermon over him
Said that "his soul had risen on the notes
Of the grand anthem which he had inspired,
And having reached the Music all divine
Had softly sunk, as light is lost in light,
Into the pure Celestial." Here he stopped.
Men were great preachers in the olden time.

It happened that a certain Giannolo,
Facchino Bergamasco, or a man

From Bergamo, a porter by his trade,
Who carried heavy burdens, yet withal
Was not o'erburdened with a load of wit,
Hearing this sermon, got it in his head—
And no great wonder either—that the late
Departed bellows-blower must have been
The Chief Musician of the Holy House;
And knowing that the man who bloweth up
A pair of bagpipes also is the one
Who plays upon the same—drew inference
That the deceased was the true organist,
And he who played thereon his humble aid,
Who only worked to keep the tune in time.

Now being smitten with a deep desire
To rise in life and also to be called
A Child of Art—with a nice salary—
And have a sermon preached o'er him when dead,
Giannolo unto the Bishop went,
And made a great entreaty to be placed

Among the holy followers of Saint Mark,
And that the aim of his ambition was
Alzare i mantici quando su-
onava gli organi—that's to say:
"To lift the bellows when the organ played."
And as he was a stout and lusty knave
Who might be useful in a hundred ways,
They gladly took him on, so there he stayed
Blowing the bellows faithfully in time.

I ween there is not in all Italy
A man—unless he came from Bergamo—
Who could have blown an organ seven years
In the full faith that he was playing it,
And was indeed the real organist.
Yet this, in fact, unless the legend lies,
Was what befell Giannolo. By this time,
Having laid by a very handsome sum,
And being well attired though modestly,
As is becoming to a Son of Art,

He went a-visiting his native place,
Where all who were related unto him—
That is to say about one-half the town—
Did greatly marvel at his handsome clothes
And at his air of stately dignity,
But most of all when he informed them that
He was no more a porter: he had felt
Immortal longings in him to arise
Above that vulgar calling, and to soar
"'Mid palpitations sweet and pleasures soft,
The manifestations of that beauteous life
Diffused unseen throughout eternal Space"
Which men call Music; and that he had risen
Even to a monthly salary of ten francs,
Wherewith were many pleasing perquisites;
And that he played the organ in Saint Mark's,
As all the world allowed, in perfect time.

Uprose a buzz of strangest wonderment,
Or, as 'tis writ, *Di che restarono*

Più maravigliati; for they all
Were much amazed that such a common man—
Si vile e si rozzo—such a boor—
Had risen to the pinnacle of Art
In Venice, where all Art was at its height,
And gained the crown of glory—*Iddio!*
"Ten francs a month besides the perquisites!"
They bowed before him with deep reverence,
Hoping he'd stay with them a little time.

Then some one spoke with hesitating tone,
As if in fear to take a liberty,
And said: "Your Excellence—if we might dare—
Since we would celebrate the kind return
Of such an Honour to our noble town,
Would you not grace the occasion, and increase
Our joy and sense of deep respectfulness,
By playing Vespers for us in the Dome
On Sunday next?" Giannolo bowed low,
And in a speech adorned with many flowers,
Which he had culled from sermons in Saint Mark,

Acceded gracefully to their request,
And said he would be there to play, in time.
When Sunday came there came with it a crowd
Such as Bergamo never saw before,
For in her streets and past her palaces
Thousands in holiday attire swept on,
And even afar there was a thundering roar,
From time to time, which rolled from square to square,
As when the incoming ocean, with a tide
Urged by a tempest, breaks among the rocks.
Yea, there were many—*tanto popolo*—
All that the church would hold, and then outside
A vast, impatient, brilliant multitude,
Such as had ne'er been there at any time.

And at the appointed hour Giannolo came,
Rising before the people in his state,
Waiting awhile the appearance of the man
Who was to play the organ while he—blew!
And all the congregation waited too,

All staring steadily at the great man
In anxious expectation, till at last
Giannolo from the pulpit cried aloud:
"Where is the man who is to touch the keys?
What is the use of making music, hey—
And filling up the thing with melody,
As I have come to do, unless there be
Some one to click the bones and let it out?
You don't suppose that I can raise the wind,
And steer, and sail the ship as well, my friends.
Such things were ne'er beheld at any time."

There was an instant's silence—deep and strange;
In all the great cathedral rang no sound.
All stared at one another open-eyed,
Or at Giannolo—just as if some power
Before unknown in life had seized on them
With a tremendous sense of dire amaze,
Not knowing what the devil it could mean;
When all at once they *took*—and from them all

There rose a roar of laughter like a crash
Of thunder, and so near it that one seemed
To miss the lightning—or, as I might say,
'Twas like a flash of sound—and then again
It came re-echoed from the multitude
Gathered outside, as the electric peal
Resounds, repeated by the mountain tops.
Yea, such a peal of laughter as the book
Declares "at vespers ne'er was heard before,"
And ne'er again will be at any time.

Moral. I pray you think upon it well.
There are full many people in this world
Who think that they are wondrous wise in ART,
And who, as Critics, write about the same
In transcendental phrase with capitals,
And call it Faith, and Love, and Heaven knows what,
And cannot think of it without a gasp
And uttering phrases silly, mystical,—

Because they are the empty, windy ones,
Inflating and inflated, who but blow
The bellows of the organ, yet believe
That they are leaders in the Realm of Art!

THE GOTH AND THE PIGEON

AMONG the merry tales of olden time
Which are still current in fair Italy
Are many told in taverns or in type
About the rude barbarians of the North
Who cross the Alps, even as they did of yore,
When they invaded fertile Lombardy,
And helped themselves to all which pleased their eyes,
And paid for it in iron and with blood:
Those times are fled, but Northmen still are here;
States fall, arts fade, but English yet abound,
And Austrian-Germans and Americans
Stalk proudly through the streets with Baedeker,
Or Murray, with the very gait and air
Of their barbarian ancestors—although

They are cleaner washed and more completely shaved—
Bet high upon the latter ; for as once
They came to rob the natives of their goods,
The latter now do live by spoiling them.
And thus strange things do happen in this world.

Thus we may note that all these foreigners,
Be it the daintiest English dame alive,
Or damsel born in fair America,
Or Russians of a royal family,
Or Frenchmen of the very noblest stock,
Or Viennese as elegant and *fesch* [1]
As even Viennese can be produced—
Wherein they wellnigh rival Baltimore—
Are still regarded by the Italian with
A doubtful smile, who as he smiles exclaims :
"*Sono forestieri*"—which indeed
Means "They are foreigners"—and yet the word

[1] A very peculiar Viennese slang word, signifying stylish or elegant. It is supposed to be an abbreviation of the mispronunciation of the English word fashionable—*Germanicé, feshionable.*

Comes from *Foresto*—savage—desert—wild—
And so do ancient thorns live round the rose.
And thus strange things do happen in the world.

Now it befell that in the Lombard time
When Dieterich-Theodoric was king,
And from Ravenna ruled all Italy,
The court religion was the Arian,
To which men nowadays an Unit add,
Yet do not add by the process—that I see—
Aught to its value; but the odd result
Was that the Gothic warriors nothing knew
About the mystery of the Trinity,—
Nay, they were even far more ignorant
Than was the English curate, who when asked
What he did understand by the Holy Ghost,
Replied: "I am not sure, but I believe
It is a kind of pigeon." These poor Goths
Had never learned so much as this youth knew.
And thus strange things do happen in the world.

Now it befell that once a Visigoth
Stately, while all unconscious of his state,
And proud while nothing thinking of his pride,
Went stalking onwards through the streets of Rome,
Unheeding all the casual passers-by
Who turned to look at him—as a grave bull
Might walk through many sheep—or as my lord
Guy de Plantagenet just now walked by
Before my window, where I writing sit,
In Florence—true he came *bien à propos.*
And thus strange things do happen in this world.

Well then, this fierce barbarian from the North,
Who as I said was densely ignorant
Of Trinitarian theology,
Was not much further in the Italian tongue,
Seeing that that which he essayed to speak
Was of the *pidgin* kind,—oh, marvel strange!
Oh, wondrous miracle!—lo, how the Muse
Brings up that word to keep me to my tale!
Ah! what strange things do happen in this world!

Now as he strode along the Roman street,
With thoughts of dinner flitting through his soul,
Lifting his eyes he saw upon a sign
The picture of a dove with outspread wings
Above the door of a *trattoria*,
Which means a place where you can treat yourself
To what you want—that is, a restaurant.
And 'neath the bird he read inscribed in gold:
Spirito Santo; and he gazed at it,
And took an object-lesson, and exclaimed:
"So *that* is the Italian for a dove!
I must remember it." So in he went
Repeating ever to himself the words
"*Spirito Santo! Santo Spirito!*"
Those who o'erheard him deemed him a devout
And fervid follower of the Trinity.
And thus strange things do happen in the world.

And having sat him down, the waiter came
And asked His Excellence what he would have;

To which his Gothic Excellence replied:
"I want a bottle of your noblest wine,
With it a soup of highest quality,
And after that a roast San' Spirito!"
"A roasted—WHAT? Signore," cried the man,
As one who had not rightly understood,
While all the guests around did glare amazed.
"I said," resumed the Northern warrior,
"A *Spirito Santo*, such as you have got
Upon your sign outside—a *bird*, you know,
That moves its wings like this"—and here he moved
His bended arms like wings, both up and down,
While with his voice he murmured *Coo-oo-oo!*
Or what is called in French a *roucoulement*,
Or *girren* in the German. Hearing this,
All who were present promptly understood;
And though they all were naturally polite,
And never laughed at any foreigner
Before his face, because he erred in words,
This was too—too—too much, and all burst out
In a tremendous—an Homeric roar.

They drew the line at pigeons ; and the Goth
When 'twas explained laughed loudest of them all ;
And thus it was he learned another word.
And thus strange things do happen in the world.

REFLECTIONS IN A PRINTING-OFFICE

FAUST means a fist—a fist can hit, I ween:
Faust made the greatest hit that e'er was seen.

I know not if 'twas Guttenberg
Or Faust who first began
To print—the honour was too great
For any single man.

Printing is called the Art of Arts,
And typos then are artists—right—
They are the nobler counterparts
Of those who work in Black and White.

APPENDIX

ORBUS IN TACTU MAINET.—P. 2

THERE were in Philadelphia, forty years ago, two sailors' groggeries in Water Street, both having the sign of The Boy and Barrel, derived from the infant Bacchus. One of these had for motto the words exactly as here misspelt and divided.

TIME FOR US TO GO.—P. 64

In one of his admirable papers, "At the Sign of the Ship," published in the *Cornhill Magazine*, Mr. Andrew Lang, in discussing Sea Songs, wrote the following :—

"In an unpublished play by Mr. Henley and Mr. R. L. Stevenson, a play called *Admiral Guinea*, that veteran ruffian, Mr. Pew of Treasure Island, makes his appearance. He has been a sailor of Admiral Guinea's in the slave trade, and he haunts the evangelical and remorseful Admiral like an evil conscience, singing snatches of the following 'Slaver's Song.' Mr. Henley has kindly copied out the whole piece, which was published in Mr. Leland's 'Captain Jonas Fisher' in *Temple Bar* about fourteen years ago. Whether the ballad is traditional and collected by Mr. Leland, or whether to himself is due the great credit of the authorship, I am not aware."

Truly I am not the author of the song which I picked up in Philadelphia before the War, nor do I know who wrote it. I am tolerably certain, however, that I, having slightly retouched it, republished it in *Temple Bar* as quoted. There are, however, others besides Mr. Lang who think I wrote it, so I give it here in order to make truth known, but chiefly because it is in keeping with other specimens of sailors' lyrical folk-lore in these pages, and will be acceptable to all who like such ballads.

SAMUEL JACKSON.—P. 99

"And of the heathen natives with their suppositious wiles."

I once crossed the Atlantic in a sailing-vessel, sharing my state-room with a veteran sea-captain who had been for forty years in the whaling service. He had an inexhaustible stock of sea-folk-lore, which he freely imparted to me who was an eager listener, and as the voyage lasted *thirty-five* days I had opportunity to gather much. I am indebted to him for this amusing interchange of words. When telling me that he once went incognito to revisit his old home in Connecticut he said, "I passed under a superstitious name."

THE END

Printed by R. & R. Clark, *Edinburgh*

THE

POETICAL WORKS

OF

SIR WALTER SCOTT, Bart.

Selected and Edited, with Introduction and Notes,

BY

ANDREW LANG

In 2 vols., Crown 8vo, Price 5s. in Cloth; or 6s. Half-Bound

Uniform with the Dryburgh Edition of the Waverley Novels

ADAM AND CHARLES BLACK,
SOHO SQUARE, LONDON.

www.ingramcontent.com/pod-product-compliance
Lightning Source LLC
LaVergne TN
LVHW010214110826
845151LV00004B/1077
* 9 7 8 1 4 2 5 5 2 7 6 5 5 *